Early
LITTLE FEET BE CAREFUL

Little Feet *is enthralling from beginning to end . . . an irreverent, refreshing story woven throughout with pathos.*

– Rev. Dr. Martha Jackson Oppeneer

Bauer-King's brilliant shaman-like exploration of life, death, love, pain, gods and goddesses embarks on a quest for a new way to navigate this patriarchal world.
Sometimes painful, often bittersweet, always funny.
Nancy Bauer-King cuts through the madness of the pandemic, global warming, and conspiracy theory politics to uncover the raw memories and simple truths of life with clarity and humor.

– Jennifer Rupp, author of the *Highlanders of Balforss Series*
(as Jennifer Trethewey)

Nancy Bauer-King's writing is unlike anything else I've read. The way her mind and spirit navigate life and prose is transcendental and magical, and at the same time, solidly grounded in reality. In Little Feet Be Careful, *she zeros in on personal intimate moments of her life, and by doing so, she opens the door to our universal, shared experiences. Her questions are our questions. Her journey enlightens us to the journey we are all on.*

– Constance Malloy, author of *Tornado Dreams: A Memoir*

I've been accused of not having a religious bone in my body. I take this as a compliment. Spiritual bones, maybe—religious, no. Nancy Bauer-King's fiercely honest explorations of her own faith in Little Feet *have encouraged me to reopen doors I thought had closed long ago. I was also drawn in by her musings on old age, her fraught early years, and caring for her dear husband, Charlie. Nancy is a wise, compassionate, pee-in-your-pants funny woman – a "crone" in the best sense of that word. You'll learn a lot from her.*

– Carolyn Kott Washburne, Adjunct Associate Professor Emerita, Department of English, University of Wisconsin–Milwaukee

Nancy invites us to listen in on her search for wisdom to make sense of her journey as a woman in a Trumpian time. This is a woman's search for voices of vitality in a man's world. Recommended for anyone looking closely at their soul's journey.

– Reverend Dr. Don R. Francis

Poignant, witty, and wise, Nancy Bauer-King shares stories of her grief during her husband's memory loss and subsequent death. She invites us to explore our relationship with the Divine, through her lifelong search for the Divine Feminine. At age eighty, Nancy is a wise and gifted guide who can help each of us to keep searching, in our own way, for our essential connection with Holy Mystery.

– Reverend Dwight H. Judy, Ph.D., Professor Emeritus of Spiritual Formation, Garrett-Evangelical Theological Seminary, author of *Embracing God: Praying with Teresa of Avila*

To: Sarah & Alex

Some grandmothers sew quilts
for their grandchildren. I stitch
words into stories.

Merry Christmas — 2021

Much love,

G. Nancy

Little Feet Be Careful

Nancy Bauer-King

Ten|16
PRESS

www.ten16press.com - Waukesha, WI

For information, please contact:

www.ten16press.com
Waukesha, WI

Editors: Kim Suhr and Carolyn Kott Washburne
Cover artist: Jayden Ellsworth
Art Director: Kaeley Dunteman

For Brenda, Linda, Mary Ann, Jim, Don, Cari, Lea, Nikki, Nicole, and Brian, who served as midwives for these pages.

Little Feet Be Careful

September 30, 2018

"Where do you want to sit?" my husband, Charlie, asks. We are on our way to church.

"Toward the back," I answer. "Near the toilet. My high blood pressure pill kicks in about 9:30."

"Do you care which side?"

I consider. On sunny days, the stained-glass windows that circle around the ceiling of the sanctuary let in the morning sun. As the capricious beams dance across the pews in a rising arc, people on the right side don sunglasses to keep the rays from singeing their eyeballs. But today is gray.

"No," I answer. "I don't care which side. It's clouded over. We won't be blinded by the sun."

And, there it is. *Blinded by the Son.* Groping in the shrouded dark for decades. Still bound in patriarchal ligatures.

Vi and Ron greet Charlie and me as we walk into the testosterone temple. Jeff hands us a bulletin. The Gospel lesson is Jesus healing Blind Bartimaeus.

I make it through two Father/Son, he/his hymns before I have to take my 78-year-old bladder into the restroom. I dawdle until the benediction.

* * *

"We ask two questions throughout our lives," the seminary prof said. "Who am I? and What am I for?"

His eight-word claim thirty years ago took up residence in the hard wire of my brain.

My answers keep changing.

In less than two years I'll be 80. How am I going to survive as an old woman in a patriarchal culture with a husband who is losing his memory?

* * *

"Where are we?" Charlie asks as I park the car. "We're at First Church," I answer again, dismayed that he doesn't recognize the building. He follows me to the west entrance and through a door he entered six days a week for over a decade.

"How long was I here?" Charlie asks.

"Eleven years," I answer. We have driven to Kenosha to drop off an article about the church that we in found an old magazine in Charlie's files.

Pastor Sue comes out of the office to greet us and is pleased to have the 20-year-old article. We visit for a few minutes about the people we knew when Charlie was pastor, some of them dead, some still leaders. Charlie listens and nods. "How long was I here?" he asks again in a lull in the conversation. He raises his eyebrows in amazement when I answer.

"We're standing in the Charles Bauer-King room," I say, and lead him a few steps to the column where the plaque is displayed. He smiles and stares at his name. The room is a large space for gathering after worship, coffee, fellowship, storytelling.

He doesn't remember that the room was part of a $1.5 million renovation that he oversaw during his tenure as lead pastor.

He doesn't remember his retirement party, the gifts, the hugs, the tears.

We're walking back to the car when my husband asks, "How long was I here?"

"Eleven years," I answer and make sure we're both belted in before I start the car for our drive home.

* * *

First Song #1

Little feet be careful
where you lead me to.
Anything for Jesus
I would gladly do.

My mother, one of the Sunday School helpers, decides I need to sing during the Children's Day Sunday School program. The other five-year old Nancy joins me. People smile and clap when the short ditty for Jesus is done.

Properly tied in white lace rules, I try to be careful where my little feet go, but a couple years later, while I am cavorting in the small patch of grass in front of the church between Sunday School and worship, my sandaled feet lead me into a hidden pile of dog poop. My mother says I do not have to go to worship. I skip the seven blocks home. Gladly. And wash the dried poop off my new shoes without gagging.

That excremental blessing is the only time I am excused from church.

Every other Sunday, *every Sunday* of my childhood, my father insists the family attend Sunday morning indoctrinations. Because my parents are in the choir and my baby brother is in the nursery, I sit alone in the third pew from the back of the sanctuary. To my left, a scowling, stained-glass Jesus acts in loco parentis. When I'm not singing hymns or listening to Reverend Anderson's lugubrious intonations about Father God, I study Jesus' feet, which are standing on a rainbow and are the same fleshy peach color as his face. His sandals and toes are outlined with black swirls of some kind of permanent pigment. And in this window the Son of God has only four toes on each foot. Imagine. Not only can the Son of God walk on water and balance on a rainbow, he can do it with missing digits.

In Sunday School I hear stories about this towering figure of Jesus. How he and his disciples walked miles and miles over dusty roads healing people. I notice that his feet are still squeaky clean. Obviously, wherever Jesus' feet led him, he was *very* careful.

Our Lord and Savior would never step in dog poop.

* * *

"Selling Christ!?"

I'm surprised when I see the title of a pamphlet Charlie is tossing onto a recycling pile. I point to the thin, tattered publication.

"Are you throwing this away?"

He shrugs. "I don't want it."

Caught by the title—bad theology in Old English type—I pick up the yellowed-with-age imprint. Lydia Davis, Charlie's mother's maiden name, is hand-written in perfect Palmer Method penmanship over the subtitle—*A Message of Vital Importance to Young People.*

I open the pamphlet.

. . . We're running around with the Devil six days a week and trying to keep company with the Lord on Sundays. That don't go with Jesus. He is not going to play second fiddle, so don't you fool yourself. Jesus says, "If you are not with me you are against me." But that's the game we are trying to put over on Him. Give the Devil the best of your life and give God the rest. He don't want them. He wants your youth, your strength, vitality and very issue of your life.

The paragraph gives me hives.

I can almost overlook the grammar of the author, Mr. Harry W. Vom Bruch, but as I flip through the 32-page diatribe against "fleshly desires, card-playing, dancing, and theater – all sweet enticements designed to send a participant straight to hell" I can hear my father's commanding voice.

"No drinking. No smoking. No sex before marriage. No dancing, card playing, or movies on Sundays."

My father and Vom Bruch's restrictive and joyless god captured my "youth, strength, vitality and very issue" of my life for way too many years.

I rip the pamphlet in two and toss Mr. Vom Bruch's sales pitch into the recycling bin.

* * *

"I don't want to do Jesus anymore," I say, sitting in one of Don's office chairs. My friend is the pastor of the church Charlie and I have attended since our retirements. Don has heard my theological drivel before and doesn't argue or try to talk me into some kind of ecclesiastical obedience. In the short time I've known him, I've learned to trust him implicitly.

"What *do* you want to do?" Don grins and swivels his chair to face me.

"I don't know. I'm tired of the preponderance of male pronouns. The creeds. The hymns. All the time. Father this. Son that."

Don nods. Sighs. "How can I help?" he asks.

"I'm not asking you to change anything. I know what happens. Change *trespass* to *sin* in The Lord's Prayer and you have to deal with an uprising from the pew."

Don runs his right hand through his full head of white hair.

"Actually," I continue, "I'm tired of the story. I've heard it my whole life, preached it for over 30 years. It always turns out the same. It's meant to free me up, but I feel trapped."

Don is quiet for a moment and then asks, "What other story do you have?"

Crap. I don't have another story, and I want one. One with an old woman technophobe who is trying to survive in a patriarchal culture.

* * *

"Santa Claus is a fictitious character," my father says, apprehending my childhood magic. He coaches me to say *fictitious* without lisping so he can show me off and get a laugh from the people at church. I grow up not believing in Santa but *really* believing in Jesus.

I believe the little baby Jesus *really* sleeps through all the "glorias" and "alleluias." I believe the grown-up Jesus *really* walks on water, stops wind in its tracks, and heals people with spit.

I believe everything my father tells me.

Then a few years ago, on a trip through Turkey, the tour bus stops in Myra at a church that our guide says was served by Saint Nicholas.

What? There really *was* a Santa Claus?

After walking through the sanctuary and sitting in St. Nick's throne chair, I go into the gift shop and buy a little red-and-white bag of "healing" dirt dug from the church grounds.

If there really *is* a Santa Claus, does that mean there really *isn't* a Jesus?

Just in case, I tape a few grains of that holy dirt in every Christmas card I send that year.

* * *

Eufeminism

She/he
tee hee
all the men have missed her

God's wearing
ruffled shirts
and calling me her sister

A-men
Oh men
if you'd live in glory

He who has
ears to hear
listen to our story.

* * *

I'm tired of the Jesus story. Not only does it always turn out the same, but the whole account is focused on self-sacrifice from the male point of view. Isn't there a story of a strong woman who chooses whom she loves, makes decisions about her fertility, and confronts inequities out of love?

A woman whose life illustrates the full unfolding of her gender?

And gets in trouble, of course.

I want another story.

Maybe a goddess. Not some beauty like Venus, who popped full grown nude, balanced on a shell, with her flowing gold hair covering her crotch. Or Athene, who sprang from Zeus' head after he swallowed her mother, Medusa, writhing poisonous snakes and all.

I don't want to replace God's son with some Jesusina goddess who emasculates men.

I don't want to worship any gender.

I want a story about the fullness of a dark womb holding secrets. Chthonic amniotic fluid that births babies and spins stories about baking bread pudding, sewing kitchen curtains, and being trapped in a house trailer washing rape off the walls.

* * *

Most of us are dragged toward wholeness.
— Marion Woodman

* * *

Rusty and I meet for lunch. I'm 38, recently graduated from the University of Wisconsin-Zero and trying to decide how to use my useless Independent BA degree in Religion and Psychology. Graduate School? Seminary?

"I wrote to Joseph Campbell," I say after we order.

"Why?"

"I said I'd read his paper 'Schizophrenia: The Inward Journey.' Told him about my psychotic break and how important his paper was. How I didn't feel alone anymore. Asked if he had any advice about a career."

"Did he answer?"

"Yes."

"Really? What did he say?"

"Not much. It was a short letter. He said maybe I could find something that would help people who have experienced the same kind of *trip* I experienced. Not young people. Adults. He mentioned Big Sur."

"Ah. I've been there. Beautiful place. What else did he say?"

"He thanked me for the kind words I said about him. I didn't want him to offer me a job or anything."

We're quiet when our food arrives. Three bites into my salad, I say, "I've been thinking about Campbell's hero journey."

"And?"

"The guy leaves home, slays a dragon, gets a gift, and if he doesn't die from third-degree burns, goes back to his community and shares the gift."

"Yes?"

"That's a man's story. What about a woman? What would be the steps in a *heroine* journey?" I grab an extra napkin, get out my pen and am ready to make a list.

"Blood," Rusty says. "There's always blood."

I laugh. "Right. Periods. Births. Babies."

Rusty tears off a piece of hard roll and says, "Having children *is* an important piece. I have a friend who said her life was going well until she had babies. She felt like a diaper fell over her head. She's 53. Her kids are grown and gone. She says the diaper is still there."

I laugh and see those cloth diapers. The Curity samples with little blue flower designs that came as a prize in a box of detergent. The flowers that got covered with gaggy, yellow-green poop.

Childbirth. A definite heroine step. I write childbirth on my folded placemat and am ready to list another woman journey step when we are interrupted by someone Rusty knows.

* * *

*In the beginning was the Word, and the Word
was with God, and the Word was God.*
— John 1.1

* * *

"Look Charlie!" I interrupt my husband, who is reading the latest Dirk Pitt novel, to show him the picture splashed across the front page of this morning's *New York Times*. "It's the first ever photo of a black hole."

"Oh." Charlie raises his eyes long enough to glance at the newspaper. Eager to share my excitement, I summarize what I've read. "It took years to get this shot," I explain. "Telescopes all over the world, hundreds of astronomers collecting data."

Charlie nods.

"Listen to this quote," I say, trying to keep my husband's interest. "Shep Doleman said, 'We have seen what we thought was unseeable.'"

"Who's Shep Doleman?"

"One of the astronomers, who described what he saw. Like a giant eyeball."

"Oh."

Charlie is more interested in rescuing Dirk Pitt from another peril than caring about the voracious void.

But the black pupil surrounded by a fiery-ringed, yellow-orange iris sucks me into Bible verse wordplay.

In the beginning . . . the earth was a formless void. Genesis 1.

Formless void? Sounds like the black hole.

What about the Gospel Writer John's assertion—*In the beginning was the Word*? John is making a case that Jesus is God's Word made flesh. But where did he think the *Word*—and his words—come from?

And Jesus in the flesh? Where did *he* come from? John has obviously forgotten about Mary and her anatomy.

Later, when Charlie and Dirk Pitt are safe again, I share my musings about the black hole and the Bible.

"In the beginning was not the Word," I say. "In the beginning was the Womb."

Charlie, used to my irreverence, doesn't blink but quickly comments, "Isn't *womb* a *word*?"

"I know. Absurd."

But, where do my words come from? Where is the prompt that prods me to make some kind of sense out of the chaos that careens through my synapses, presses my fingers onto a keyboard, and pushes out a river of words that talk back to me when printed on a page?

Creative ideas must bubble up from a formless void. A churning chamber of birth.

* * *

In the beginning there was nothing. And, God said, "Let there be light." And, there was light. There was still nothing, but you could see it a whole lot better.
— Ellen DeGeneres

* * *

"Schizophrenia: The Inward Journey," a paper by Joseph Campbell gave me my first hope for overcoming my psychiatrist's summary at the release of my first hospitalization: *prognosis for psychotherapy quite poor . . . pattern consistent with a psychotic individual.*

I became a Campbell fan and tried to fit my life into the plot of his hero journey.

Leave home.

Face some kind of dragon.

Win and be given a boon.

Return home and share boon with community.

I left home, fought demons, learned everything is a story, and shared stories of hope and love for over 50 years. But I'm still fighting a male world dragon, a world in which the Green Bay Packers' score, the Dow Jones average, and the price of gas is more important than an ice shelf the size of Rhode Island that just broke off Greenland.

* * *

Now that I'm old and retired and try sitting through church, I can't decide what to do with Jesus. How can I follow him if I'm minus the "extra finger" that dangles between his legs? The powerful appendage is never mentioned in the Gospels. No one reports Jesus "turning aside," the Hebrew euphemism for taking a leak. How could he wander all over Palestine healing lepers, quelling storms and resurrecting dead people, without having to find a tree or shrub at least a couple times a day?

And sex? Who knows what went on under those tunics?

* * *

My mother said having a baby is like having a hard bowel movement. I believed her.

* * *

My first child was born during semester exam time for her student-father. He drove me to the hospital, waited three hours far far *far* away from my screaming, and then passed out on the floor next to my foggy groggy bed. After the nurse let him get off the other bed, he left in a hurry to take a math exam. He returned in the evening with a dozen red roses.

My first bouquet of roses ever.

Due on Christmas day, my second child was induced, and both the doctor and I made it home for the holidays.

My husband presented me with six red roses.

Three-hundred sixty-four days later, another Christmas due date, another doc with holiday plans, another induction. But this time there was too much pit too fast, sudden anesthesia, a ripped cervix, an internal stitch job, several bottles of IV fluids, a third child . . .

. . . and three red roses.

My fourth child was born a month overdue, luckily nowhere near a major holiday, but in the middle of the sale of our house and packing to move across country three weeks after his birth.

My husband, whose vasectomy had healed, presented me with one red rose.

A plastic red rose.

I was 23.

* * *

Stan, my then-husband, and I are undressing in his bedroom. It's 8:30 we're back from our Dubuque elopement and more than ready for legitimate intercourse. I peek at the nest of forbidden fruit he has kept hidden in his boxer shorts. How could something so exciting look like the turkey neck in a sack of giblets?

* * *

In my next life, I will not allow my mother-in-law to take charge of my reproductive life. Still in high school and enrolled in Whitewater State Teachers College in the fall, I acquiesce when Marian says I need to be fitted for a diaphragm.

Too frightened to ask what a diaphragm is, I wait for the appointment she made for me with her gynecologist in Madison.

Dr. Schuette is a stout, 50ish woman, wearing a maroon gabardine suit and a creamy colored blouse with a ruffled jabot that spills like a waterfall over her pillow chest. After introducing herself and showing me into a brightly lit room she says, "Sit here in this chair next to the counter. Before I examine you, I'd like you to look at this model of a woman's anatomy so that you'll have a better understanding about the placement of a diaphragm."

The plastic model, about the size of a cantaloupe, has been cut vertically to illustrate what my sex parts must look like. Dr. Schuette explains the birth control method my mother-in-law has chosen for me by naming each reproductive organ and moving her finger through the garish pink ribbed piping.

"Do you have any questions, Nancy?"

I shake my head. I am 18. Never have had the courage to look "down there."

Dr. Schuette nods, tells me she needs to examine me, and to undress from the waist down. She gives me a skimpy gown and leaves.

I squeeze my eyes shut during the shock of cold metal and Dr. Schuette's mantra, "Just relax. Just relax. I'm almost done."

Directing me to sit on the edge of the examining table, the doctor snaps open a white container and lifts out a pale circle of rubber the size of a Miracle Whip jar lid. Referring to the half-sex-parts-model, she reminds me how the round stopper is supposed to slip up the vagina and fit snugly against the cervix. Then she squeezes an inch of wormy white goo onto the tiny frisbee and says, "I'd like you to try and put this diaphragm in place. The best way is for you to squat on the floor, press the edges together slightly, and push it in with your fingers."

What? I have to do this in front of her?

"I'm going to go into my office while you practice," she says. "Will you be okay?"

Relieved that she is leaving, I slide off the examining table and follow her directions.

The domed cup slurps right into place.

I hate the thing. I'm always aroused before remembering the cap, and by the time I go to the bathroom closet, pry open the container, squeeze out the spermicide and pop the prevention into place, I have to start all over again with the touching and rubbing part.

Although I use that diaphragm religiously, several determined little sperm slip around and under. Our fourth child is born a month after our fifth anniversary.

* * *

Creativity happens in the realm of the mothers.
— Carl Jung

* * *

What other story *do* I have? Pastor Don's question stops me cold. I don't have another story. And I want one. I want a story that unfolds to reveal the ultimate fulfillment of a *woman's* life. Not a male. Like Jesus. Definitely not like my Sunday School Jesus. Rabbis were married, which means Jesus probably left his wife and kids to run around the countryside with a bunch of men. Maybe he was gay. Savvy man that Jesus was, he probably allowed Mary Magdalene to trail after his crew to dispel any notions about his sexual inclinations.

But what other stories? Maybe a goddess story. Who were those feisty goddesses who showed up in my Ancient Near East Religion course?

Tiamat. Split in two by Marduk. *She won't help.*

Ishtar. Sex *and* war. *An oxymoronic Lysistrata?*

16

Isis. *Ah. Yes.*

Her story includes resurrection *and* a virgin birth! She finds out that her husband, Osiris, was hacked to death by his jealous brother. She locates all his body parts except his penis, which had been thrown into the Nile. Not a problem for Isis. She turns into a kite, flies around him, collects his seed, and gets pregnant. A virgin birth.

Isis is a possibility, but I might end up on a terrorist list.

And this story doesn't include forgiveness and grace.

Wait. If I don't believe everything I do is either wrong or not good enough and get loaded up with guilt, I don't need a story that includes forgiveness and grace.

* * *

Guilt, the gift that lasts forever.
— Rusty McKenzie

* * *

Except for the hours the small room is used for group therapy, no one in the psych unit seems to mind if I play the upright piano that hugs the corner near the door. On the second day of my second hospitalization, Rusty walks through that door while I'm playing "Nobody Knows the Trouble I've Seen." She apologizes for interrupting me, introduces herself, and invites me to attend art therapy.

Although humiliated at being hospitalized again, I'm curious about art therapy and like Rusty immediately because she apologized for interrupting me. And she didn't demand that I attend.

She invited me.

Throughout my 65 days in St. Elizabeth's, Rusty offers me paper, pastels, markers, crayons, and her counseling skills. She encourages me to draw the demons that show up trying to kill me, and one afternoon she lends me her power to fend off one of the evil specters.

"What's happening, Nancy?" Rusty sits next to me on the closet floor.

"I'm scared."

"Of what?"

"What I was drawing." I bow my head in shame.

"The demons?"

I nod. "A red one."

"Can you talk with it?"

"NO!"

"Why not?"

"I'm afraid of it. It wants to kill me."

"Talk to the demon."

"I can't! It wants to kill me!"

"We know what the demon wants. Now tell it what *you* want."

"I want it to go away!"

"Tell the demon to go away. Tell it."

"Go away." I am mumbling softly with my eyes closed and chin resting on my knees.

"Can you speak up . . . so the demon can hear?"

"Go away!" I say with more volume. Feeling stronger, I look up. The demon steps back and then fades into the wall behind my bed.

Finally. A protective mother. A mother who lent me her power long enough for me to get a sense of my own.

* * *

2004

On the fifth day of the Crossroads of Turkey tour, our guide stands at the front of the bus and says, "We'll have an hour in the Museum of Anatolian Civilizations. It's a new museum in Ankara and has excellent displays of antiquities. Be sure to return in an hour. We have a five-hour ride to Cappadocia."

I'm tired of on-the-bus-and-off-the-bus with lots of other people on this tour. I'm tired of mosques, carpet factories, and shish-kabobs. I'm tired of standing in a line of women to use the facilities.

Still irritated at waiting 10 minutes to use the museum rest-room, I find my husband, Charlie, looking at a book in the gift store, and we climb a few steps to the beginning of the historical artifacts. As usual, Charlie heads off at his own speed, wanting to see everything. Glad to be alone, but weary and disinterested in old things that all look alike, I amble past headless statues, stone pots, and ancient utensils.

Then I round a corner into a diffused golden lit room and see her. Hannahannah. A grandmother goddess, sitting upright on a terracotta chair. Her bulbous breasts spread out over a corpulent belly. Her arms rest on the backs of leopards. Two spotted sentinels watch me warily.

Hannahannah. A seventh century BCE goddess, discovered by archeologists in Catalhoyuk.

Hannahannah. Older than Mary, Diana, Astarte, Cybele. Isis.

Back in the gift shop, Charlie buys the book and I find a clay replica of Hannahannah. The small Grandmother Goddess fits in my hand and my suitcase.

19

* * *

"See you in church," my retired colleagues say as they leave our condo.

"I don't do Jesus anymore," I say. I stick out my index finger and add, "You know, when the guru points at the moon, the disciples don't look at the finger."

Probably because they are bundled up and halfway out the door into the cold afternoon, the only responses I get are wan grins.

Tired of worshiping an idol and bowing my head in a Protestant slump to petition for something in Jesus' name—as if the name itself is an Open Sesame God for everyone at all times in all situations—I want to sit in silence, wait and watch for moon mystery to show up.

* * *

A woman asking for equality in the church would be comparable to a black person's demanding equality in the Ku Klux Klan.
— Mary Daly

* * *

November 2018

Charlie and I join a few dozen other theatregoers in the Milwaukee Repertory Theatre's Quadracci Powerhouse Theater for REP in Depth, a half-hour pre-show of tonight's performance of *Miss Bennett: Christmas at Pemberley*. The dark-haired young man on stage at the microphone will provide extra information about the production. He wants audience participation.

20

"How many of you have read Jane Austen?" he asks. Most hands go up, including mine. Another question quickly follows. "How many of you have read *Pride and Prejudice* or seen it on stage?" I read *Emma*, but can't remember reading *Pride and Prejudice* or seeing it on stage. Fewer hands. Not mine.

The actor is animated and fires more questions about the characters until only two people are left raising their hands. Satisfied that he knows his crowd, the actor focuses on Jane Austen. The era she lived in. Her culture. Social courtesies. Civilities. Behaviors. How her writing dealt with power issues. "Stultifying time," he says. "She was confronting the place of females in her culture. We can compare it to the #MeToo Movement. She was subversive," he says and grins as if subversive is an okay thing.

Subversive? When I confront, challenge and rage at religious stuckness, am I being subversive? While the speaker continues to describe Austen's writing, I'm savoring the word subversive. Sucking on it like a Werther's caramel hard candy. Swallowing the smooth butter cream sugar.

Sweet.

* * *

Me Too Counting

Can I count the man at the healing workshop who insisted that if I had never been loved by a black man I didn't know what love was really like and then stuck his legs out straight between his desk and my chair so that I would have to crawl over or under his legs to get out of his office?

Can I count the slimy church member with greasy gray curls

who licked his lips and said I was such a pretty girl, then pulled me behind the heavy doors to the sanctuary and stuck his frothy tongue down my throat? Oh that's just Les, the pastor said.

Can I count the six-foot-two, 225-pound husband who squeezed both of my hands together in one of his meaty fists and with the other pulled me down the hallway threw me on our bed unzipped thrust zipped up again and left for work?

Can I count the men who drive the trucks with bug shields that read Midnight Wonder, Scream Dream, Metal Pecker and rumble past the United Methodist church I serve?

Can I count the 1500 centuries that God's Name is only Father, so therefore a father and lots of males like Earl Len Stan Roy Harvey Al Garrison Matt and, of course, Donald think they must be God?

* * *

"Did anyone else in our family have depression?" I dare to ask my mother.

"No." She hesitates, then says, "Well, there was Crazy Aunt Lu."

Who? What? I've never heard of this woman. My middle name is Lu. "Who was she?"

"Oh, she was Kimble Killam's sister."

"My great grandfather? The guy who was superintendent of the insane asylum?"

"Yes . . ."

"What happened to her?"

"I don't know. Her brother locked her up at Rock County and she spent her life there."

My mother is staring at me. Does she hear my heavy intake of breath?

Suffocating dark. Room 508.

Does she see my twitching eyelids?

Dim light through barred window in locked door.

Though improbable, I must ask. "Was I named after her?"

"No. Of course not," Mother scoffs.

My question opens the Who am I? What am I for? locked door again.

Again.

Again.

* * *

I Google Hannahannah and read information provided by Wikipedia, brittanica.com, and Godchecker.com. She's an Anatolian Grandmother Goddess and was among a number of terra cotta female statuettes discovered in the archeological dig at Catalhoyuk in the late 1950s. Though sources agree that she was a Mother Earth figure—a personification of nature, fertility, creation, and destruction—there is no clear relationship to other Ancient Near Eastern goddesses.

Theologians think Hannahannah is a minor goddess. Evidently old goddesses are like old women. We don't count for much.

* * *

Rusty and I meet at Victoria's on College Avenue. As soon as we've ordered, I ask, "Remember that lunch when we agreed Campbell's hero journey described a male's life and we tried to come up with steps for a woman?"

"Yes?"

"And then I found the Maureen Murdock book . . . "

"What was the name of that again?"

"*The Heroine's Journey: Woman's Quest for Wholeness.*"

"Right. I remember you showing me."

"I was excited about her book. I think I was on the second step. Something about identifying with the masculine."

"And?"

"I was fascinated with her list, but I didn't finish the book. I got bogged down half way through."

"So?"

"Well, I just found the book again. Guess what the sixth step is."

"Yes?"

"Initiation and descent to the Goddess."

"And?"

"I'm so there."

* * *

There are hundreds and hundreds of goddesses. I skip the already familiar Greek, Roman and Ancient Near East goddesses and get lost in exotic names of dozens of sacred representations: Niger-Congo Nana Baluka; Quechuan Axomamma; Shinto Izahami no Mikoto.

On and on.

Many divinities are figures of both creation and death—the womb and tomb thing—but I quickly catch on there are three major goddess types: virgin, mother, or crone.

I'm pushing 80 years old and have limited time to find help in this techy, Trumpy world, so I omit the *always* beautiful virgins (what do they know about bladder leaks and a-fib?) and frenetic mother goddesses (too busy wiping snotty noses and chauffeuring kids to soccer practice).

I go right for the crones.

Crones, as discussed in www.goddess-guide.com: *associated with the words crown, wisdom keeper, seers . . .*

So far so good.

. . . old age, death, winter, doomsday, waning moon, crow.

Crow. Crown. Potato. Potah-to.

* * *

Cybele: Great Mother of the Gods, whose story starts somewhere in the ancient world. A couple of centuries before Jesus, a sacred black stone representing this goddess was brought in a triumphal procession from Phrygia to Rome. Her worship included killing a sacred bull, who represented Attis, her dying-god consort. The highlight of the worship was baptism in the blood of the bull.

Of course, Christians took over Cybele's religion. By the fourth century CE, they had replaced her temple with St. Peter's basilica and *watered down* the baptism ritual. They kept the dying god and blood, but instead of killing bulls, they stomped barrels of grapes and drank the fermented product until they were sotted with ecstasy.

* * *

"This is the Body of Christ," I say, holding up a hunk of bread that looks and feels like yesterday's brat bun.

What am I doing here?

". . . broken for us," I continue, and because the communion stewards have already cut a vertical slice in the bun from the bottom, I easily twist the stale body of Jesus into two pieces without grimacing and tugging.

I turn and put the broken Body of Christ on the paten and lift up the cup of grape juice.

"This is the Blood of Christ, shed for us," I say and raise the chalice.

Grape juice? Ha. A collaboration between the temperance movement in the late 1800s and Mr. Welch, an entrepreneurial Methodist. And Cybele, the old goddess, is still present.

What am I doing here?

This time I'm here because the pastor is on vacation and he needed someone with the "right sign" across their forehead to officiate at this sacrament. He knows I'm tired of Jesus-the-male who has been turned into an idol.

And I don't believe Jesus died for *me*.

He was killed because his radical belief in an omnipresent *loving* god (instead of a distant *perfect* one) pissed off Jewish religious leaders and Roman prefects.

The *Jesus died for your sins* thing? A theology fashioned by early church "fathers" who figured out how to keep the institution going. Insist on a bunch of impossible to keep religious rules. Offer forgiveness for mistakes. Break more rules. Need more forgiveness.

Voila! A vicious circle that's been spinning for almost 2,000 years.

I want out of the circle *and at the same time* I want to be in a group of people who believe in something greater than we are.

A mystery.

Makes my head hurt.

Especially on Sunday mornings.

* * *

Mother starts in before we're even seated at the table.

"Don't you think the pastor's wife ought to be in church?"

Shit. Here we go with attacks on the pastor's wife.

"Doesn't she have a job in Madison?" I ask.

"Yes. She's a nurse."

"Do you know her shifts?"

"No."

"Maybe she works nights. She'd have to drive an hour after work to get here."

Why am I defending the pastor's wife? I don't even know her.

"I don't know *when* she works, but she certainly wouldn't have to work every Sunday. She could get here at least once a month. She doesn't come at all."

How do I get pulled into these conversations? What is this cauldron of hot bile that wants to bubble up and spew at her? Is her anger at the pastor's wife an oblique attack on me?

What does my mother want from me?

* * *

You don't have to participate in every argument you are invited to.
— Source Unknown

* * *

There's always blood. The male hero slays the dragon if he's lucky and maybe drags a bloody steak home for supper. Female blood signals she is ready to gestate life.

27

Pregnant over half of my first five years of marriage, the Modess box of 48 sanitary napkins gets dusty in the bathroom closet. After my husband's vasectomy, potential life slips away each month with relief. Years of routine "monthlies" follow with no thought of ever conceiving.

Then at 45, the bleeding becomes heavy, as if red flagging a desperate last chance for another child. I'm reminded of my stubborn resistance to fecundation on significant—even sacred—events.

While I kneel before the bishop at my ordination.

While I serve communion the first time.

While I repeat wedding vows with Charlie.

Each time a blatant dressing down that I am a woman and don't belong in a profession reserved for men.

* * *

Frank, a member of the congregation I serve, has submitted a petition to get rid of all United Methodist clergywomen.

Obviously I am a huge disappointment to Frank. He doesn't like the hymns I choose. He doesn't like my preaching. He tries to enlighten me by stopping in the office during the week with books, magazine articles, and newspaper clippings that reinforce his conservative theology.

"What experiences have you had that lead to your beliefs?" I probe during one of his office confrontations.

"The Bible!" he declares vehemently, astonished at my implied apostasy. "It's the TRUTH!" he adds, as if he is speaking in stained-glass calligraphy.

Though Frank has clear opinions about homosexuals, drunkards, and abortion providers, he is closemouthed about his own life.

From the congregational grapevine, I learn he is 50ish, single, and works for a trucking company. On Sundays, he is dressed neatly in a suit, dress shirt, and tie. His gray hair has a natural wave and is parted in a sharp, straight, line.

Frank's displeasure with me has not affected his involvement in the church or the community. He is generous in his donations to the hospital and food bank. He contributed land for the expansion of a county facility, but he wants his gift to be anonymous and doesn't want any money spent on beauty products for women.

Until I heard the rumor about his petition, Frank has been patient with me. His petition, however, is a head-on challenge. At my request, he agrees to bring the petition into the office.

Although our greeting is amiable, I don't know whether his florid complexion is due to anger, medication, or religious fervor. Without further conversation, Frank hands me two sheets of paper, sits down in the chair next to my desk, and folds his arms across his chest to wait.

The petition begins:

> I feel it has come time, and so do many others, that there is a much needed change in the Methodist church. We need to get <u>men</u> back into the pulpits, we aren't learning anything and our minds are everywhere but on the message. You must accept what scripture says in regard to this matter.

The petition continues with extensive single-spaced quotes from 1 Corinthians 14, 1 Timothy, Hebrews, and Galatians; each chosen verse relegates women to a subordinate and often silent role. *He* and *men* are underlined wherever they occur in the text.

Frank adds his own comments in between biblical invectives:

God chose his <u>men</u> to write the Bible.

There are some very good <u>men</u> preachers on television.

Finally, I want to state I am not anti-women.

29

My spirits sag lower and lower as I read. How am I going to respond to this? Frank won't want to hear that his petition will be ignored or laughed at by the church hierarchy. Ignored.

He sits quietly until I finish reading his petition and hand him back the pages.

"This isn't personal," Frank says to me. "Behind the desk you're okay," he concedes, "but in the pulpit, *no way!*"

I can't respond. Frank is intent upon getting rid of me as a pastor as well as getting rid of my ordained clergy status. How could it not be personal?

Seminary professors advised, "Just love the people." I knew what they meant, but I had cared about Frank through hours of conversation for six years with no indication that he was interested in anything but his narrow-minded crap. I was tired of loving him.

"I know you feel strongly about this," I say, pointing to the papers in his hand and hoping to bring an unresolvable conversation to a close. "I'm probably not going to change my mind. My experience is that there are many images for the Holy One. There is a quote I use: Not to call God 'father' is unbiblical. To call God only 'father' is idolatry."

"God is a MAN!" Frank screams and slams his fist down on the arm of the chair.

Startled, I remember to breathe. Obviously this man has a limited capacity for metaphor.

"I guess we're just going to have to agree to disagree," I say when I've recovered from the shock of his outburst.

"No, we're not!" he announces and pushes himself out of his chair. With his petition in hand, he leaves, slamming the door behind him.

* * *

During homiletics class, the prof reads a quote from Walter Brueggemann's book *Finally Comes the Poet: Daring Speech for Proclamation*. When he finishes, a woman in the front row raises her hand and asks, "What's a metaphor?"

Anything you want it for is my snarky and silent answer. How did this woman get through all her schooling without knowing about metaphors, similes, synecdoches?

I buy *Finally Comes the Poet*.

Six months later I'm kneeling in front of Bishop David Lawson, who is stretching out his hand to put the holy seal of ordination on my head. Draped behind Bishop Lawson is a 20-foot banner with the inscription *Take Thou Authority* in huge, cream-colored letters.

From her seat in the balcony, Rusty takes a picture of the transformative moment.

I laugh when she gives me the photo.

The imposing figure of Bishop Lawson blots out the last three letters in the banner.

Take Thou Author . . .

"It's a sign!" I say to Rusty.

I like thinking of myself as a poet and author. Aren't I cradling metaphors when I hold the bread and grape juice for communion?

* * *

"Go get your mother," my father says, his hands on the steering wheel of the '46 Chev. I slide my eight-year-old body out of the car and pull open the heavy door into the church. My parents are often among the last people to leave after Sunday services, but Mother is not in the narthex chatting with Lorraine, nor at the coat rack straightening empty hangers. I hurry up the steps to the sanctuary door and see her sitting in the second pew from the back of the church. She is already in her shapeless gray, wool, winter coat and one of those funny little knit hats (this one was navy blue) with an attached fur covered U-shaped head band that clings tightly to her head and frames her measured face.

She is the only one left in the sanctuary.

Before I can announce that my father has the car pulled up and waiting in front, I see Mrs. Anderson, the pastor's wife, in her purple paisley dress coming through the door by the organ. Sun shining through the Jesus stained glass window highlights Mrs. Anderson's wavy white hair and soft, powdered, pink cheeks.

"Why, Phoebe, are you all right?" she asks, approaching my mother.

My mother stands up, nods her head, and, wincing with embarrassment, answers, "I gurgled all over everything."

Gurgle? *Gurgle?* What's the matter with my mother? I'm only eight years old, but I read a lot. Gurgle belongs to the rippling sound of bubbling brooks tumbling over rocks. Or gurgle belonged to my baby brother lying on his back and babbling through saliva bubbles.

Mrs. Anderson reacts quickly to my mother's plight. "Oh . . . oh, Phoebe. Can I help? Can I get you something? A hand towel?" Mrs. Anderson's words are kind. Sweet. No hint of alarm.

Gurgle? What's the matter with my mother?

Then I see my mother's legs, the few inches that aren't covered by her long coat. On the outside of her right foot, I see a thin string of blood trickling dark red down her stocking toward her shoe.

The sight startles me. Stops me from speaking.

"I'm okay," my mother says, shrugging her shoulders as if resigned to what is happening. "I'm just waiting for Russell."

Mrs. Anderson sees me.

"Oh. There's Nancy."

Without a word of explanation, Mother joins me. We walk down the church steps, out the door, and get into the car. My father drives us home through a strained silence. My fear settles into fascination. I have witnessed a mystery reserved for adults. Questions about grown-up secrets that are taboo.

* * *

1950

My cousin, Phyllis, married Chick on a sunny, late summer day on the front lawn of Uncle Johnny and Aunt Esther's large, creamy brick farmhouse.

Before the wedding, when Phyllis asks my father to sing "I Love You Truly" and "Because," my father refuses. He thinks his voice is getting too scratchy, but after my cousin pleads with him, my father compromises. He'll make a 78 rpm of the songs, bring the record player to the wedding, and play the renditions.

Because Phyllis has asked me to pour the punch, my mother makes me a new dress out of white eyelet and a crinkly light blue fabric. I am 10 years old and feeling very grown up.

We get to Aunt Esther's early on the big day so that my father can get set up. With our card table on the lawn to hold the record player and electrical cords unwound and stretched from the house through the grass like thin, black snakes, he is primed and ready for his solos. But when the time comes, my father has trouble with the cords and volume.

He can't get the record player started right away, and when he finally gets the disc spinning, his voice is scratchier than his normal voice.

However, I pour the red, sparkly punch without spilling a drop on my fancy new dress.

After refreshments, aunts and uncles and cousins from both sides go inside to watch Phyllis and her new husband open their gifts. As Phyllis unwraps towers of white paper and ribbons, the "oohs" and "aahs" expressed are sometimes drowned out by my overweight Uncle Harold's booming voice.

Just as the unwrapping is nearly complete Uncle Harold bellows, "Well, Phyllis, I suppose the next pile of gifts you open will be for a baby!"

As chuckles ripple through the downstairs, Uncle Harold's comment evokes in me a mysterious sequence I have already noticed—marriage first, then babies.

My curiosity peaks as the room is quieting down for the last unwrapping. I turn to my mother and ask, "Why don't babies come until after you're married?"

Uncle Harold explodes into a sharp clap of laughter. "Yeah, Phoebe," he roars to my mother. "Why *don't* babies come until after you're married?"

I know by my mother's flushed face I have said something terribly wrong. The whole downstairs is holding its breath waiting for my mother's reply. Mother is looking down at her hands and twisting her rings.

"God just plans it that way," she finally answers.

While Phyllis and her new husband finish opening their new life together, I imagine an old, wrinkly man with matching long white hair and bushy eyebrows opening a heavy, black book and deciding it was time to send Nancy a baby.

Later that fall, during fifth grade recess, I learn that evidently God needs some help dispatching babies.

* * *

Kenlyn Shaw, a big eighth grader, catches up with me as I'm walking home from school. I'm surprised when she stays in step with me and even talks with me, a mere seventh grader. I'm even more surprised when Kenlyn tosses her soft auburn curls and turns our conversation into talk about boys and sex.

We've crossed the bridge over Saunders Creek and are on the sidewalk passing the Lannon stone pavilion at the edge of Edgerton's Central Park when Kenlyn giggles and says something about a boy using a rubber.

A rubber? One of those black things my mother used to make me pull onto my shoes when it was raining?

Afraid I'll appear stupid to Kenlyn, I nod knowingly. A few weeks later, during a sleepover with my friends, I learn what rubbers *are*.

At 16, I learn how rubbers *work*.

* * *

Summary of my 1950s sex information: *Sex is dirty. Save it for someone you love.*

* * *

Mother is leaning over the kitchen sink peeling carrots. I'm hurrying past her for a date with my steady boyfriend, Ronnie. She interrupts my exit. "You know," she says without turning to look at me, "babies don't come from the stork." Startled at her rare and oblique reference to sex, I mutter some response and get out the back door. Quickly.

Mother's caustic caution was six years too late. My repertoire of reproductive facts began during a fifth-grade recess when my friend Susan called me over to the chain link fence that bordered the playground and gave me my first sex ed lesson. Wide-eyed with excitement she said, "My mother is going to have a baby and my sister told me what happens. My sister said that my father had to stick his thing into her."

I didn't have to ask what his *thing* was and was stunned speechless with the repulsive information. Susan cracked the silence with more upsetting news. "The mother has to drink the father's pee, and sometimes fathers do it to their little girls."

That night I lingered in the clawfoot bathtub, folding the washcloth into careful quarters, dipping it into the lukewarm water and holding it over my belly. I watched it drip, drip, drip onto my naked tummy. What awful thing was going to happen to me?

To her credit, when I turned 13, Mother did open a door to "the talk." Except she didn't talk. She walked across the living room floor and without speaking and handed me a packet of pamphlets she must have sent for from a Kotex or Modess ad. She didn't wait to see my cheeks turn crimson. She walked back to the kitchen, and I ran upstairs to my bedroom clutching my embarrassing puberty.

The pamphlets explaining "those certain days," were advertising propaganda. Illustrations in the Modess tract are of a young girl in blurred and muted colors of gray, brown, and dirty yellow. In each picture, the girl, sprawled across a bed or chair, looked at the pamphlet in her hands with downcast eyes as if her pet cat Muffy had died. In the last picture, she was holding a box of 12 and studying it like a fortune-teller's globe revealing nothing in her future but the curse of being female.

Again, Mother was too late with her "facts of life" help. During slumber parties, my girlfriends and I had giggled our way through pilfered prurient reading material. To my relief, drinking pee wasn't mentioned anywhere, and instead of repulsive, the *thing* became strangely fascinating.

Mother's warbled warning about storks and my boyfriend, Ronnie? Way too late.

* * *

Costas, our tour guide, is standing in the midst of ancient columns and speaking to weary and almost ancient travelers. He points to a statue of a woman who is minus some of her face and an arm. "Astarte," he says. "Then she was Diana. With a progression of male usurpation, she became Mary."

I roll my eyes. Sigh. Quietly.

* * *

I'm going to stick with Hannahannah, the grandmother goddess. The oldest of them all. She lived several centuries before Jesus' mom, Mary. Hannahannah's daughter's name was Mari. Her son's name was Same-el. Funny. The biblical Hannah had a son named Samuel and Mary's mom was named Anna.

Coincidence? No, say the theologians who have studied for years so they think they know everything. They say the names evolved from the Hebrew *Channah,* which means *grace,* and the Semitic *Anat* means *water spring.*

But weren't these folks nomads? Wouldn't these ancients have bumped into each other at an oasis on a trade route? Wouldn't they have told grace-filled stories around a water spring?

And what's more grace-filled than finding water in a desert?

* * *

Grandmother Goddess lives in a white house with cinnamon smells. Makes me brown sugar sandwiches. Plays rummy with me. Reads me Donald Duck and his three nephews—Huey, Dewey, and Louie—stories from dawn to dusk. We pick raspberries in straw hats to ward off sun and bugs. Fill our buckets with soft red pulp. August breezes puff through open windows, fluff lace curtains over the maroon mohair couch and my dreaming childhood.

* * *

The Goddess Guide lists 38 crones. I look for Hannahannah. She is not listed. Nor is Ereshkigal, who sounds cool but hung her older sister Inanna on a peg and left her to rot and die.

In her positive aspect, a crone is often depicted as a grandmother, a wise woman, or a midwife . . . whose knowledge is sought out to guide others during life's hardships and transitions.

Ha. What knowledge? I'm not needed if Google is available.

Wisdom? Everything I've learned was through reflection on my own experience. Even if someone seeks me out, they are searching for their own wisdom. Not mine.

Besides, *I'm* the one who is searching for ways to survive decrepitude. And so far these old goddesses aren't much help.

* * *

December 2008

Janine, Brenda, Helen, and I each drive from our respective corner of the state to celebrate an early Christmas in Portage in a room at the United Methodist church. Although we've been good friends and meeting every few weeks for 30 years, we haven't been together since September. We spend a couple hours catching up on our lives, our kids, and our plans for the holidays.

After we share gifts, Helen picks up a book she brought and reads a poem about the annunciation—the angel Gabriel telling Mary she's been chosen to bear God's son. Finished with the poem, Helen closes the book, puts it on a table at her side, and says, "Mary is an object of devotion for me, especially in her obedience to God."

Through the years, Helen has occasionally shared her loving regard for Mary. Although always troubled by Mary's effortless acquiescence to holy orders, I've been quiet out of respect for my friend's steady devotion.

Until now.

"I can't buy it," I say, and immediately regret breaking the reverent silence. Except for her stare and raised eyebrows, Helen's face is motionless. Janine and Brenda look down at their hands folded in their laps.

Finally Helen asks, "Why?"

"I don't know. Something about Mary's just rolling over. No pun intended. I mean, a strange guy with wings swoops in and tells her she's going to be pregnant? Not with any old kid, but the son of God? She had to have been freaked.

39

I continue: "I know. Gabriel says, 'Don't be afraid.' Easy for him to say. Angels always say that just before the lucky receiver gets his or *her* life upended."

Helen doesn't argue with me. She restates her belief that Mary personifies a faithful woman, one who surrenders to God's plan. Janine and Brenda are quiet. Someone notices it is lunchtime, and soon we are on our way to a nearby restaurant.

At the time, I didn't know the reason for my strong reaction against Mary's unquestioned submission. Now I do. I'm upset that the men telling the story didn't include any internal turmoil the poor woman might have had.

Did she weigh the consequences? (Stoning)

Did she wonder if she had a choice? (Evidently not)

Did she pull herself together in time to fetch water, make dinner, do the dishes? (Of course—she's a woman)

The Mary story evokes the anger I swallowed during all my years of submission to men and a male god without knowing I had a choice. I just rolled over. Figuratively and literally.

* * *

"Mary was probably raped by a Roman soldier."
— My clergy friend, Tom

* * *

February 13, 1970

The leader sits at the head of tables formed into a U shape and welcomes 26 people to the Ecumenical Institute. He briefly shares the plan for the Religious Studies 1 weekend and invites us, beginning with the person on his left, to go around the table and introduce ourselves by name and where we're from. Nancy Ore I say . . . someone quips "or what?" . . . and I add Appleton, Wisconsin, into the laughter.

We go around the table again and share our religious background. Life-long Methodist, I say. I don't say my parents bound me tightly with a list of nos:

No alcohol.

No smoking.

No swearing.

No sex before marriage.

No playing cards on Sunday.

No play until all the work is done . . . and the work is *never* done.

The leader says, "We'll go one more time around the table. This time imagine your tombstone. What are the dates on it? What is the epitaph?"

"March 14, 1980," I say, stunned that I am only giving myself 10 more years of life.

"And your epitaph?" the leader prompts. "What do you think will be written on your tombstone?"

I mumble, "I don't know."

"Well, what do you think summarizes your life?"

"I can't think of anything," I say. Maybe my face must signal distress, because the leader doesn't push me for an answer.

* * *

A great silence overcomes me and I wonder
why I ever thought to use language.
— Rumi

* * *

The Fuller Brush man kneels on our living room carpet, opens his case, and begins his pitch. Mother, interrupted from doing the laundry in the basement, is settled on the overstuffed, rose-colored chair. She leans forward and scans the household cleaning products spread out on the floor in front of her. Because she hasn't objected to my presence, I watch while the gray-haired salesman lifts brushes and bottles from his display and explains the wonders of each product.

Although Mother rarely buys anything from door-to-door peddlers, she is in no hurry to return to the basement. After she looks page by page through a proffered catalog, she finally points to the open case in front of her and buys a scrub brush the size of my teacher's blackboard eraser.

As she gets up to find her purse, the salesman stands, shakes out his pant legs, reaches into his suitcoat pocket, and pulls out a tiny plastic tube about an inch long.

"Here," he says to Mother as she gets up and steps past him. "A thank-you for your purchase. A sample lipstick."

"Oh. No." My mother shakes her head and continues to walk toward the dining room table. "I don't wear lipstick."

"How about your daughter?" the salesman asks and turns to give the prize to me. Tantalized, I hold my breath, expecting my mother's refusal. But at that crucial moment, Mother is rummaging through her purse.

Preoccupied, she doesn't answer.

Within seconds, I have the promise of an exciting future nesting securely in my right hand. Before Mother has paid the Fuller Brush man, handed him his fedora, and shown him out the front door,

I'm upstairs in my room with the lipstick and already creating my defense to a certain argument with my father, who has been clear about his disdain for women who use *face paint*.

Several times in the presence of both parents, I have asked my mother, "Why don't you wear *any* makeup?" Several times my father has answered, "Your mother has an *inner* beauty."

Does his go-to statement mean she's ugly?

At supper, my father, whose teacher's salary doesn't allow for any frivolities, asks my mother about the new scrub brush on the kitchen counter.

"I bought it from the Fuller Brush man," she says. "He was here this afternoon." Mother clears her throat, looks over at my father, and adds, "He gave Nancy a lipstick. A sample."

"Oh?" My father looks at me.

I quickly swallow the piece of meat loaf I'm chewing and launch into my arguments. "Can I wear it, *please*? I'm 13 now. You said I could wear nylons and heels for my confirmation. Can I wear lipstick, too? Just a little bit? The color is real light."

My father puts his fork down and stares at me.

Anticipating a stern *no*, I stupidly blurt out, "Marilyn's mother said *she* could wear it."

I know what he's going to say before he says it: "If Marilyn jumped off the bridge, would you jump off the bridge, too?"

But he doesn't say it. And I don't say anything more either.

Sometime between that supper and my promise to follow Jesus for the rest of my life, my mother's inner beauty must have persuaded my father to let me have a little taste of adulthood.

On Confirmation Sunday, he saw my painted lips—my *lightly* painted lips—and didn't say a word.

* * *

"Why are you going to seminary," Rusty asks. I'm surprised at her question and give a snarky answer, "I just want to get out of Appleton."

I'm confused. Rusty seems confrontational, not curious. Raised Catholic, Rusty calls herself a born-again pagan. Sometimes when I'm talking about church or Jesus, she grimaces and waves her hand in front of her face like she doesn't want to hear me.

Nor see me either.

I answer Rusty more carefully. "I had to deal with that question several times on my application. They bought the faith-y reasons I came up with. But I really don't know why I'm going. I think I want to do the Bible stories for myself. And I want to be near holy things."

"What do you mean by 'holy things?'"

"Well, you know. Weddings and funerals. Important rites of passage. And communion, too. Only ordained clergy can do baptisms and communion."

Rusty stretches out her hands, looks at her fingernails for a few moments, and then says, "I thought you were going to go to your friend's farm and watch him slaughter his cow. Did you?"

"No . . ."

"Why not?"

I can't answer. Where did I read about the crowd holding their breath at a bullfight? I can't remember the word for the heart-stopping silence in that slim slice of time between the life and death of the staggering animal.

"I don't know why," I answer, admitting my defeat. "I don't think I could bear watching a mortally wounded cow fold into its legs and collapse."

"Wouldn't that be a holy moment?" Rusty asks.

* * *

First Song #2

Little feet be careful
Where you lead me to
Anything for Jesus
I would gladly do.

My little feet led me to semen-ary and right into sin. My roommate—another 40ish mother of several kids—and I did a late adolescence.

*We rescued a "No Bull-shit" sign from the dumpster and in the dark of night taped that critique above the professor's podium in Room 205, the largest lecture hall.

*We stole the broken finger from the third floor forgotten Jesus statue and gave our colleagues the finger.

*We had a weekend affair. Well, my roommate didn't do the affair thing. She had a happy marriage.

Someone said Garrett-Evangelical Theology Seminary was a crucible. Turned out my 48-hour affair was alchemy. My whole body glowed gold.

* * *

Through the stained-glass Jesus window of my childhood, I see the side of Erna Boettcher's house. Miss Boettcher is the head librarian at the Edgerton Public Library and has a voice like gravel being scraped across a dishpan. When I tiptoe into the musty building, she glares at me through black, round-rimmed glasses from her raised desk at the front of the room.

Rules are absolute. No noise. No gum. No candy.

When I find the latest Nancy Drew mystery and approach the desk, Miss Boettcher plucks a pencil from behind her ear without disturbing even one of her carefully rippled gray waves. With deft no-nonsense movements, she removes the yellow card from its sleeve in the back cover, writes the due date on both card and sleeve, and hands the book back to me.

How old was I when my best friend, Sarah, the pastor's daughter, took me into the library stacks, plucked out *For Whom the Bell Tolls*, led us out of Miss Boettcher's sight, and opened to the sleeping bag scene?

Or the Sunday afternoon when Sarah talked me into ringing Miss Boettcher's front doorbell and giggle-dashing back behind the church?

Who knew sin could be so delicious?

* * *

My Christology final included my learned definition of Jesus Christ: the center point of a turning world. I included a short description of my locked-in room experience. Dr. Redmond gave me an A, but I knew from my suicide attempt that the center *isn't* Jesus. The center is a bottomless pit. A black hole. A swirling abyss from which I grabbed onto the name "Jesus" as I was being sucked into psychotic oblivion.

Just the name. Jesus. The name that had been washed over my brain at baptism and every Sunday and every every *every* Sunday thereafter.

Weekdays, too.

I still don't know why I participate in a worship that has turned Jesus into an idol instead of a man whose life provided an option (*one option*) for successfully navigating over and around the black hole.

Is there a woman whose name will help me?

Women in the Bible? Not Mary, who acquiesced to giving birth to a god without asking even *one* question. Not Hannah or Esther or Ruth. All good women, but coopted by men.

Hmm . . . There's Jael. She saved her people by driving a tent stake through the skull of Sisera, a Canaanite commander.

I like her style.

* * *

We drift on legends forever.
— Euripides

* * *

When our ancestral *fathers* in the faith wrote Genesis, they omitted Adam's first wife, Lilith. Nomads, they obviously met weird people from other tribes at the wells and must have been intrigued by strange stories of gods *and* goddesses, especially the Sumerian goddess Belili. The divine lady.

Why not give Adam a wife? He's been screwing the animals and "wasting his seed." A huge sin. God wanted *his* people to "go forth and multiply." Sodomy and masturbation meant precious semen was lost. A definite sin.

In addition, the proscribed position for sex was *missionary*. Or *heaven over hell*.

47

Lilith (Hebrew for Belili) would have none of it. She sneered at Adam, cursed him, and flew away to the Red Sea, where she copulated with demons and gave birth to 100 children every day.

Which explains some of our current national turmoil.

Depending upon which story you like, God made Adam a helpmeet. Eve. His second wife. We know how the rest of that story turns out.

Obviously the men were in charge of telling all the stories. They scapegoated Eve. And I'm still trying to get "out from under."

Anyway, the "lily" keeps showing up. Easter. Mary's favorite flower. And there's the story that when the Angel Gabriel came to tell Mary she was "favored" by God and would bear a son, Gabriel was carrying a lily with God's semen in it. Gabriel poured it into Mary's ear. Which kept her hymen intact. A virgin.

Why didn't I tell these stories from the pulpit? The folks might have had more fun.

* * *

Who told me about Maureen Murdock's *The Heroine's Journey*? According to her circular representation of steps in the journey, I'm almost 80 years old now, and in Step #6, "initiation and descent to the Goddess."

The next step? "An urgent yearning to reconnect with the feminine."

Is my *yearning to reconnect* with the feminine the driving force in this search for a goddess? Shit. I don't have time to reconnect with the feminine. I'm not sure I have *ever* been connected.

* * *

LITTLE FEET BE CAREFUL

The woman sitting at the restaurant table across from me rummages through an expensive leather purse the size of a saddlebag, lifts out a pocket mirror and two shiny silver tubes that she lays on the placemat in front of her. Holding the mirror carefully in her left hand, she pulls a black-tipped brush from the thinner tube and with her right hand begins to outline her lips.

She catches me watching as she twists the cap off the fatter tube; I look away. When I dare to peek again, her lips glisten bright red.

Her artistic application is a mystery to me. No one taught me about makeup. My father cited some biblical injunction against women adorning themselves, and my mother easily agreed with his disdain of all face paint.

When my father pronounced, "Mother has an inner beauty," he didn't describe Mother's hidden attractiveness.

Pissed because Revlon kept changing my favorite shades, I quit wearing lipstick decades ago. The only makeup I use is for my eyebrows. Gone with all the rest of my hair within a few months of my grandson's death.

Today I went to Walgreens to replenish my one piece of face paint and discovered that makeup *makes up* an entire aisle. Overwhelmed with the number of ways to enhance one's face, I walked slowly past the strange array of merchandise. Foundation. Blush. Gel. Eyeliner. Eyeshadow. Brushes. Pencils. Brands. Products I never heard of and wouldn't know how to use.

I found the eyebrow powder and brush and picked it up. Finding myself near a display of lipstick and remembering the woman in the restaurant with her mysterious applications, I stopped to read the names: Pretty 'n' Pink, Dragon Fruit, Coco Razz, Plump it Up.

I was in a foreign land. I didn't know the language.

* * *

Who was that short, blonde, and thin woman who came for coffee with Debbie? I'll call her Rita. She sat next to Debbie on our cheap brown trailer couch, and had only had a few sips before she asked me, "When is your baby due?"

"June 21," I answered, feeling very grown up.

"I don't want children yet," she said. "Rick and I want to wait until he's finished with school."

Did I get pregnant during my first semester to escape? Maybe from the spinster who taught the required Home and Social Problems course? The one with her black hair pulled tight and twisted into a bun on the back of her head who instructed, "Don't ever serve peas in a blue bowl."

The only serving bowl I had. Blue. Plastic.

"I'm afraid to use The Pill," Rita says. "I have a friend who died. They blamed it on blood clots from the pill. I douche," she announces.

What? What's that?

"It's kind of messy," she giggles, "but . . . so far, it's working." She shrugs and takes another sip of coffee.

My grown up-ness vanishes. I look at Debbie, hoping she'll respond, but she is suddenly fascinated with the contents of her cup.

Rita changes the subject.

But what's a douche? I once overheard Junior Wescott call the school cafeteria lady a *douche bag*. Is that orange rubber grapefruit-sized bulb on the top shelf of Mother's bathroom closet a douche bag? The curved black pipe sticking out of it looks like the neck of a migrating Canadian Goose.

I'm 19. Married and pregnant, but I don't feel like a woman. Will I ever *be a woman*?

* * *

What year did Rusty drive us down to the Loop to see Judy Chicago's *The Dinner Party*? We walked into a huge room lit only by spotlights on the large triangular display. Although the designs on the plates were described as butterflies, to me, the riotous colors represented vaginal inner sanctums. I grew increasingly uncomfortable as I shuffled along the display and hurried past the last few blatant reminders of my womanhood to wait for Rusty.

Why did Rusty invite me to view this particular creation? To help me accept myself as a female?

We stopped for coffee somewhere near Milwaukee on the way home.

How did I find the courage to ask what she wanted from me?

* * *

Early one steamy August morning, I find dark red strings in my pants. I twist up the courage to go downstairs and find my mother, who is finishing her breakfast at the dining room table.

"I've started," I mumble. No other words are spoken, and I follow her to the upstairs bathroom. She opens the closet door and pulls out a new Kotex belt wrapped in cellophane and a single Modess pad from a blue-and-white package of 48. She leaves me alone to figure out how to use the belt, the accompanying pins, and the pad.

Except for the day she left the Toni home permanent in *way too long* and I looked like a Brillo pad on my first day of fifth grade, she left me alone to learn self-care.

I took care of my burgeoning womanhood a couple days after "starting" by buying my own box of 12 Kotex with babysitting money.

51

Then I met my friends at Walgreens lunch counter for our rite of passage. A five-cent Coke. Cherry Coke.

* * *

You never know when you're making a memory.
— Singer Rickie Lee Jones

* * *

"What is he doing?" I whisper to Charlie. We're in La Paz on the edge of a crowd watching a Bolivian festival. A man in a colorful striped poncho is pouring some kind of liquid onto the ground. "He's making an offering to Pachamama," Charlie answers quietly.

"Who is . . ." I begin to ask, but my husband shakes his head to stop me from speaking. Later he explains. "Pachamama is the Earth Mother. The Aymara pour beer or soda to thank her and to ask for her continued blessing. Sometimes they toss flowers or coca leaves."

Pachamama? An earth goddess? I have never heard of her, nor have I ever been in a Third World country. Charlie had been a pastor and teacher in La Paz in his early ministry, and he is eager to introduce me to a country and people he fell in love with over 30 years ago.

He is *not* eager to take me to Witches Alley. He is sorry he has described more of the sacred traditions of the Aymara people, because I want to see objects of devotion used before the Spanish rode in with their guns, germs, and sky gods. Although the encroaching religion offers a woman goddess, the indigenous folks do not allow a once-a-year Mary to usurp an everyday Pachamama.

Stepping into the Mercado de las Brujas, I'm immediately drawn into a dark otherworld and become heady with a dank, sweet smell of wet earth. Charlie, two feet in front of me, urges me to keep moving past tables and trays of dried frogs, owl feathers, small jars of aphrodisiac powders, and various sizes of llama fetuses. When I hesitate at a fortune teller's stall, he takes my hand and rescues me from certain peril.

How do I convince him that we need to buy a llama fetus to bury for luck in the foundation of our new home? He relents, pays the saleswoman in Bolivianos, and she wraps the desiccated, five-inch corpse in tissue paper.

Safely back at the hotel, I slip the fetish the color of mud into a plastic bag and tuck the body in between dirty clothes in our suitcase. I hope we can get through customs without having to surrender our prize.

We invite close friends to the ceremony. In spite of their wide-eyed stares and twisted grimaces, they join us in the ritual burial. Pachamama, generously plied with wine, blesses Charlie and me for the 15 years we reside at that home.

* * *

A myth can only be myth if you don't believe it—if you stand outside it in some kind of way. If you stand inside it, then it becomes something quite different—it becomes divine truth.
— Grant L. Voth

* * *

The baseball-sized model of Hannahannah sits on my file cabinet in front of the clay figurine that I squeezed out between my locked-up fingers in the psych unit. She reigns from the same place I put her in 2004. Guess 9,000-year-old-goddesses don't move around easily.

All the other dolls and small souvenirs that remind me of my gender, are keeping their mouths shut.

Not Hannahannah.

How could I know that when I began digging through books and websites looking for goddesses, she would wake up? That she would keep picking at the edges of my paper brain. Archeologists claim when she gets angry, she heads underground for six months and everything above ground goes to hell. Crops wither. Animals ignore their offspring. Even human mothers take time off.

For years, Hannahannah sat passive in my office, seemingly satisfied that I had carried her home in my suitcase from Ankara. But when I'd had it with Jesus and decided to look for goddesses, she dusted off her dormancy and reminded me that *she* was a goddess. A *grandmother* goddess. The oldest goddess ever dug up.

If I don't pay attention to her, she might get pissed and head underground. Then what? Would I be responsible for a global disaster?

* * *

When we recognize our spiritual daughterhood in the patriarchy, we have some excavation to do.
— Maureen Murdock, *The Heroine's Journey*

* * *

I dig backward through layers of matriarchal DNA: My mother, her mother, and mothers as far back as I have names. Strong names.

Phoebe Emogene Addie Bauer
Bessie Azelia Craig Addie Field Sellnow
Florence Mabel Chadwick Craig
Phoebe Ellen (no maiden name) Coon
Esther (no other names)

Maiden names fade four generations back, and names disappear completely after Esther. Birth and death dates are recorded except for Esther. Her given name is the only information I have. Family lore indicates she bumped overland to Wisconsin in a horse-drawn covered wagon driven by some man named Philip Coon.

Maybe she was named after Esther-the-Biblical Queen, who started out as a concubine but then became royalty after the reigning Queen Vashti said "no" to her husband, King Ahasuerus. The king wanted to show off Vashti's beauty at a party that had been going on seven days with lots of drinking. Out of golden goblets. From huge flagons.

Queen Vashti's refusal pissed off the king, and he replaced her with Esther.

And, that's only chapter one. Though the plot thickens in chapter two, Esther doesn't say no to her husband. Rather, she works around him and saves her people through cunning and political maneuvering.

Early passive aggressive.

What about my great-great-great-grandmother? While she was stumping across half of America with her husband to set up a homestead, did she ever say no? The biblical Esther gets a whole bible book named after her, while my ancestor gets a couple lines in this story.

Anyway, to me the real hero—heroine—is Vashti, the woman who said no to her husband king.

* * *

"You can't say YES until you can say NO," Rusty advised. She was referring to my acquiescence in bed with Stan, my inability to push out my breath through pursed-up lips into a clear-spoken "no."

No, I don't want sex.

No, I don't want to make a pumpkin pie for your birthday.

No, I don't want to go to your parents'. Not even one more time. Ever.

Rusty knew I wanted to say an honest yes to the man in my class at seminary.

Yes, I'll stay in the dorm this weekend.

Yes, I will go dancing with you on Saturday.

Yes, I'll come to your room after the concert on Sunday.

These days I'm having trouble saying "no" to Jesus—even though I want to. Does that mean that all those years of yeses have been dishonest?

* * *

When I married Charlie King, why didn't I take the name Nancy Queen?

* * *

I find the *old* New Testament lying on top of my grandmother's diary. The holy book is the size of a deck of cards. I open the cover and dis-cover the book was given to Phoebe Coon in 1851 as a birthday gift from her father, Stephen B. Coon.

I show the Bible to Charlie, who is putting the last pieces in his 1,000-piece Machu Picchu puzzle.

"Look what I found."

"What?"

"An old Bible that belonged to Phoebe Coon, my great-great-something grandmother."

"Where'd you find it?"

"It was just lying there on my bookshelf."

"Hmmmm."

"What am I going to do with it?"

"Eh."

The question about what we're going to do with all our ancestors' stuff has been ricocheting off the walls ever since Charlie and I began downsizing. What are we going to do with Lola Myrtle Welsh's empty spice tin? Lydia Amanda Davis' hand-painted plate? Florence Mabel Chadwick's amethyst pendant?

I look again at the old New Testament. Really, of what importance is this tattered thing? I didn't even know I had it until about 10 minutes ago. Maybe I should do our children a favor and throw it away.

Wait! Throw away Phoebe Coon? This water-stained book is the only tangible vestige of a woman who is next to the last ancestor on my list of my mother's lineage.

* * *

Charlie and I are standing on the grass in the middle of the ruins. Charlie points at Huayna Picchu and insists that I would love the view from the top. Says he's climbed it two times already. Says it's just like walking up Mosquito Hill at the nature center.

He lied.

That giant stone finger to the sky damn near killed me.

Starting out at a fit age 54, I easily navigate the first weathered slabs of Incan rock. Even the ropes, provided at strategic spots to get to the upward trail, are a cinch. The view of the ruins through the trees is spectacular. I'm not even breathing heavily near the top when the path becomes one way only.

Then, I see it. The last turn. The narrow, narrow, last turn. The necessary only 18-inches-wide last turn. And the completely unguarded edge 2,000 dizzying feet straight down to the Urubamba River. What idiot Inca had smoothed this dirt into a passage the width of a shoe box?

Taunting sirens croon from nowhere. Jump, they lure. Jump. You'll be saved. Leap of faith. Angels will catch you on their sturdy white wings.

Jump! Just jump!

I begin to whimper. Hug my quivering arms into a rough outcropping to my left. Fight off taunting sirens. Charlie, ahead of me, sees my peril. Reaches around the outcropping. Takes my hand.

Now, 23 years later, I need to hang on to Charlie as he slips and falls further into dementia.

* * *

"Would you like some coffee?" I ask Charlie.

"Are you going to have some?"

"Yes."

"Then I'll have some."

"Okay. I'll heat it up in the microwave."

"What?"

"Some coffee. You said you'd like some."

"Are you going to have some?"

"Yes. Your coffee is almost ready."

"Are you going to have some?"

"Yes. I already told you that. Three times."

"Oh. I didn't know."

"The microwave just dinged. Your coffee is ready."

"Are you going to have some?"

"Aaaaahggh!"

"What are you laughing at?"

* * *

September 19, 2018

Florence is downgraded to a tropical cyclone. The CNN reporter blames her rampage on Mother Nature. Of course. She is redflaginfrontofabull enraged at the way we continue to ravage her body.

But what about Father God? Why is the mother always blamed when shit like Florence happens?

Florence was my great grandmother's name. She was blamed for the fury that whipped through her family. Florence Mabel Chadwick was *not* related to Florence May Chadwick, the long-distance swimmer that was the first American woman to swim the English Channel in *both* directions. As far as I know, my great-grandmother didn't swim, but she did get in hot water when she was 16 years old.

The baby was my grandmother.

My mother kept the scarlet letter secret from me until after my fourth child was born. The gynecologist asked about family medical history, so I double-checked with Mother.

"Was Grandpa Craig the only one in our family who was diabetic?"

"Oh. He wasn't your *real* great-grandfather."

What!? The infant I hold in my arms has been given the name of the mustachioed man with magic pockets in his overcoat. Pockets that held pennies and lollipops and unconditional love. I tighten my hold on the infant in my arms.

"Who *is*?"

"I don't know. Your great-grandmother got pregnant out of wedlock. Her parents wouldn't let her marry a Catholic boy, and Art Craig married her to make an honest woman out of her."

What? How does getting married make a woman honest? Actually, being married increased my need to lie.

Although my Great-Grandmother Florence probably never learned the butterfly kick or Australian crawl, she did die of a *stroke*. At 49 years old.

* * *

My first husband, Stan, and I separated the same day the *Challenger* blew up. Our divorce was final on the 50th anniversary of the Hindenburg disaster.

Our older son called this morning to tell me Stan died during Florence-the-Hurricane.

How fitting.

I survived both the hurricane and the cosmic chaos of our 29-year marriage.

* * *

While my children are gathering at the airport to drive to their father's funeral, I'll be driving to my high school class' 60th reunion. The woman organizing the event telephoned a month ago and asked me to do some kind of remembrance ritual for classmates who have died. She wants my remarks to be brief. Balloons will be involved. Somehow. Unfortunately.

Conversations at each reunion are mostly stories from our school years, stories that often include the dead classmates. So I've decided to use Jim Harrison's quote from *Larson's Holstein Bull*: 'Death steals everything but our stories.'

Who knows what my classmates believe about heaven or what they expect me to say? Who knows what happens at death? I figure if my life goes on at all, it will be in the stories told about me.

Like my graduation ceremony. June 5, 1958.

"Nancy's married," Ellen hollers as 89 of us are lining up outside the gym for our procession. My math teacher father is in charge. He insists on precision and shoves off each graduating pair with left right left right in step to Elgar's "Pomp and Circumstance."

Two months earlier, disgusted at my condition, my father decreed that if I keep my marriage secret until graduation, he won't stop my elopement. I'm so besotted with Stan and desperate to flee from my father's rigid rules, I agree to the deal.

My fickle period shows up, saving me from repeating the red-letter shame of my Great-Grandmother Florence and my Grandmother Azalia (who, like her mother, was "deflowered" at age 15), but Stan and I don't cancel our plans.

For six weeks, I wear my wedding ring on a silver chain around my neck and under my blouse. As the band begins the graduation march, I whip out my wedding ring and wave it at Ellen.

My high school reunion remarks are brief. Not only because I'm following instructions to be brief, but because the sun is jamming through the too-few table umbrellas on the restaurant's steamy outside patio, and the wait staff is bringing out the food.

I'm more than ready to be *brief.*

A balloon flutters toward heaven for each dead classmate I name.

None of my live classmates mention my three-days-dead first husband.

Nor do I.

* * *

> We have to reclaim the parts of ourselves before we
> cloaked ourselves in the vestments of the culture.
> — Maureen Murdock, *The Heroine's Journey*

Vestments? Murdock means more than clothes, doesn't she? She is challenging me to dig up and divest myself of the patriarchal social mores that have tied me up and choked my voice.

But I'm thinking of clothing. Constricting clothes.

Years ago I quit wearing girdles that pinched, garter belts that chafed, and three-inch "fuck-me" pumps that threatened my balance and ruined my back. At 80 years old, I rarely wear pantyhose. After struggling into that sadistic invention, I need a nap.

Other clothing foisted on me by my ancestors were symbols of chattel.

Within days of my first marriage, my mother gave me two new, pastel-flowered housedresses with a zipper up the middle, and my grandmother gave me an apron she made with hand-appliqued figures of cacti and a man in a Mexican hat tugging on a stubborn donkey.

My mother saw my wrinkled nose and quickly returned the housedresses to the Edgerton Store. I never wore my grandmother's handiwork or an orange gingham smocked affair that I made in the '70s when cross-stitched aprons, along with bleach bottle piggy banks, decoupage jewelry boxes, and baked 78 rpm record wall plaques, became the latest fads to keep bored housewives distracted so they wouldn't try to break out of their prisons.

I keep those two aprons in an old steamer trunk underneath a faded green feed-sack apron I inherited when my grandmother died. That apron kept her housedress clean while she dressed chickens and baked pies to feed the threshers.

Murdock says I need to reclaim parts of myself still cloaked in patriarchal vestments.

I'm working on it.

* * *

I was getting ready for bed when my first husband told me I undressed like I was suiting up for a soccer game. So why, if I was such an erotic disappointment, did he volunteer me to do a striptease at his annual Rotary Club party? Betty, a school board member, and therefore technically his boss, had a Statue of Liberty costume I should wear. Over lots of laughter, they insisted I would be good at symbolizing freedom.

In those days, I didn't know how to say no.

In those days, I could have used the advice of the goddess Inanna, who had to stop and strip at each of the seven gates to the realm of the dead in order to attend the funeral of her brother-in-law. In her wake, she left a crown, beads, ring, scepter, breastplate, and royal garments.

When she arrived, I assume Inanna was clothed only in her birthday suit. Out of some pique, Ereshkigal, her jealous sister and Queen of the Underworld, killed Inanna and hung her up on a hook to rot. After three days, Inanna was brought back to life with the help of other gods and eventually freed to resume her rightful position as the Queen of Heaven.

I arrived at the Rotary Club party fully clothed in streetwear carrying a bag with the puke green Statue of Liberty outfit. The faux strip was as uncomfortably embarrassing to the onlookers as it was to me.

The faux marriage lasted 29 years.

* * *

This black-and-white snapshot was taken Christmas Day 1964. My grandmother, mother, and I are cleaning up after dinner and cloistered into the postage-stamp-sized kitchen of 705-K Eagle Heights, the University of Wisconsin graduate housing in Madison.

Grandma's hands are over the sink. Mother's hands are covered with a dishtowel, and I am in front of the stove holding a plate. I'm thin, 115 pounds. Now I'm corpulent, like my grandmother.

Whoever took this photograph is not helping with the cleanup. Whoever took this candid shot must have ordered, "Say cheese." Our heads are turned toward the camera, each face with a smile.

My smile is fake. The photograph does not include my four pre-school children, their father, or my father. Nor does it portend the future. In less than seven years, my grandmother is dead, my mother widowed, and neurotransmitters in my brain are firing uncontrolled in a locked room.

* * *

February 25, 1971

"Daddy told me not to cry," Mother says as she slides out of the passenger seat of our car and walks toward the church door.

She doesn't cry. No one else does either. My throat is tight. Teeth clenched. Don't cry, Nancy. Don't cry. Mother sits to my right at the end of the first pew on left side of sanctuary. Veryl Schubert preaches. The organist hits "All hail the power of Jesus' name." Third tune. Mother stands. My father's tenor counterpart terribly missing. I am more worried about the two children, Julie and Steve, who decided to attend than the two that wanted to stay home. Julie is next to me. Then Stan. Then Steve. The stained-glass Jesus fastens his critical eyes on me. Don't cry, Nancy. Don't cry.

What a relief when the pastor pronounces the benediction; the overweight funeral assistant shows up next to Mother and motions with his puffy hand for the family to follow the casket down the aisle. I stumble after my mother. Make it to the narthex before a choked sob escapes.

* * *

It's awful to have such smart kids and such a dumb mother.
— Phoebe Bauer

* * *

65

First Song #3

Little feet be careful
where you lead me to
Anything for Jesus
I would gladly do.

Because Mother helped in the Sunday School, she was right there to put me in the program. At home she programmed me to be a perfect Christian wife:

Worry about what the neighbors think.

Be nice.

Wear housedresses during the week. Dress up on Sundays.

Be nice.

Don't ask for anything. Give to anyone who asks.

Be nice.

Take cookies to the neighbors at Christmas.

Be nice.

Make sure the blade of knife faces toward the plate.

Be nice.

Don't cry or scream.

Be nice.

Clean everything when entertaining, including dusting off the tops of the cans *inside* the cupboard.

Be nice.

* * *

I try to explain feminist theology to women during a Bible study about Jesus and nonviolence. Thinking that these folks will be transformed by the enlightening information, and careful to emphasize that my brief explanation is only a *general* description of behavior, I draw two little stick figures with a bubble around each head, representing the ego.

"When a male is threatened," I say, while drawing an arrow that punctures his ego bubble, "he strikes out with words, fists, or weapons.

"When a woman is threatened," another piercing arrow, "she turns inward, runs or hides.

"When Jesus was threatened, he didn't fight. So women who don't fight back look like Jesus.

"Passivity is a woman's sin," I conclude and wait for the women's eyes to open wide in aha! moments, but the faces at the table are blank. So, stupidly, I try harder. "We swallow our hurt and anger and try to get our wants and needs met through passive-aggressive behavior. That's sin."

No one speaks. No one asks a question.

* * *

I'm getting into my car with a 1,000-piece Machu Picchu jigsaw puzzle from the Map and Flag Shop. The woman coming out of the next door juice bar is carrying a table lamp fastened to a slab of wood about the size of a Ouija board.

On a creative high because Jenny from "Home Instead" is watching Charlie, I hurry to get the key into the ignition, turn on the engine, and slip down the window fast enough to sing "You light up my life. You give me hope to carry ah . . . ah . . . ah . . . on . . . "

But the woman with the lamp is halfway down the block and is spared my craziness.

Debby Boone lights up my life all the way home. Her lilting lyrics keep earworm tunneling through my head as I say goodbye to the caregiver, dump Machu Picchu on the dining room table, and sit with Charlie while we separate out the edge pieces.

The nurse says the doctor wants me to take a test and hands me a packet of paper. She hesitates before giving me a pencil. A dull pencil. I promise her I won't stab myself. She doesn't laugh.

Why did I say that? Maybe this test will help the doctor put the pieces of my shattered head back together and help me learn to be a good wife. I promise myself I will answer all the questions truthfully, and I keep my promise. Until the question about hearing songs in my head. That droning must be a crazy sign. What terrible flaw is lurking that will mean prison for life?

I want to get out of this locked room. Anything to get out of this locked room.

I lie.

Why would a woman go into the juice bar and come out with a table lamp? Why would I go into a Map and Flag Shop and come out with a jigsaw puzzle? Why don't I feel anything about my first husband's death? My guru says, "Why questions are bottomless pits." Too many answers.

Debby Boone's song clogs my brain with worm scat.

* * *

Hannahannah. Are you aware archaeologists say you're a *minor* goddess? What's minor about going underground for six months? *Six months!* I can't even get 60 minutes of uninterrupted time to consider what you are trying to convey to me.

I'd like some answers. What did you do for those six months? How does a grandmother get such power? While you were lolling below, you must have known that above your head, things were really going to hell. You supposedly had more power than the gods and goddesses who were in charge of rain, sunshine, green and growing things. Weren't those royal reps pissed when the animals ignored their offspring?

How about the mothers? What did they do? Go shopping? Get their nails done? Sign up for Paint and Sip?

And speaking of sunshine: we're into *seven* months of cold and rain and dark suffocating clouds. Have you seen my rhubarb? Struggling like a half-dead roadkill just trying to put a limb out.

Three months now I've hunted for goddesses. Just like the Christian Father, Son, and Holy Spirit, goddesses come in three. Virgin. Mother. Crone. Way too many goddesses to explore in my old woman quest.

* * *

It takes a long time for one to become young.
— Pablo Picasso

* * *

Rubem Alves, a visiting theologian, is speaking in the seminary chapel. He launches into a story about his father-in-law, a German son of a Seventh Day Adventist minister who followed his religion's restrictions to the letter, including a dietary prohibition to refrain from eating animal organs.

Invited out to dinner, Mr. Alves' father-in-law particularly liked the cauliflower that was served and, when asked if he would like a second helping, said yes. "Good cauliflower," he said, complimenting the hostess as he finished. "Oh, that wasn't cauliflower," the hostess said. "Those are brains."

Mr. Alves' father-in-law excused himself, went into the bathroom, and vomited up the food.

"What did he vomit?" Mr. Alves asked a sanctuary of stunned seminarians and quickly answered his own question. "He was vomiting *words*!" Mr. Alves pronounced. "*Words*."

* * *

Charlie and I are sitting third pew from the back on the left side when Don, our pastor friend and colleague, leans into the microphone and says, "May we hear the word you have for us today." Don is praying to God—he doesn't say which god—before he launches into his sermon.

The word I hear from god is *elbow*. I like the word, elbow. Maybe God-the-Father wants me to hear the word, elbow.

I don't hear the first few sentences of Don's sermon because I'm thinking about the whole wheat elbow macaroni I bought in a fit of choosing healthy crap, and I tried it in the macaroni and cheese for comfort because my husband is losing his memory and . . . well, the whole wheat elbow macaroni and cheese wasn't comforting.

I hated it.

And I hate sitting here with all the Fathers, Sons, hes, and hims.

Hymns. My *Woman's Encyclopedia of Myths and Secrets* says that during a sacred marriage, the goddess was invoked by crying, "O Hymen Hymenae," an ancient marriage song The encyclopedia posits that cry may be the origin of the word hymn. She was probably screaming at the sharp stab of her virginity splitting.

Well, there are almost no hymns in this church with "hers." And *none* that refer to sex.

Being tired of the Jesus story brings conflict.

* * *

What is to give light must endure burning.
— Victor Frankl

* * *

May 13, 2019

Doris Day died today. According to the *Racine Journal Times*, she was 97 years old. She was like a goddess for me when I was 12 years old. When I pasted pictures of her from *Photoplay* in my scrapbook, did I know that her birthday was April 3, that her first husband beat her, or that her real name was Doris May Ann Kappelhoff?

The article says she was married four times. What was she thinking while she sang "Secret Love" during the filming of *Calamity Jane*? Was she in a secret relationship with one of the men who would become another husband?

Calamity Jane sings that she is so much in love, she can't keep the secret. Through melody and lyrics, she tells a friendly star, shouts from the highest hill, tells a golden daffodil, and wraps up the Oscar winning song with a reveal: "Now my heart's an open door. And my secret love's no secret anymore."

Thirty years after I saw that movie, afraid of a calamity, I didn't shout about my secret love. I barely whispered through turbulent May days of separation, divorce, tubal ligation, and eventual second marriage.

So what happened to my Doris Day scrapbook? Was it in the cardboard box my parents put in the attic when I left home?

* * *

Mother was 13 years old when the stock market crashed. She never talked about the Great Depression, but she ironed used gift wrap, darned holes in the heels of socks, and, for the first several years of my life, saved *every* piece of paper with my name on it.

What do I do with the box of musty grade school valentines, report cards, recital programs? Or the hospital bill of my birth?

Hospital Services	10½ days @ $3.50 per day	$36.75
Operating Room Fee		$5.00
Anesthetic Fee Ether		$0.50
Drugs		$2.00
Dressings	Mother 0.50 a day	$5.25
Baby Care	10½ days @ 0.50 per day	$5.25
Baby Formula	2 days @ 0.25 per day	$0.50
		Total: $55.25

And what about the colorful, eight-page Memento and Certificate of my Baptism proclaiming that on June 16, 1940, Reverend William S. Carr dipped his hands into holy water, dripped it on my head in the name of the Father, and of the Son, and of the Holy Ghost?

When I taught confirmation classes, I showed the bored eighth graders the artifact. None of the kids I taught seemed to care about baptism or how it was connected to confirmation. They understood they could say "no" to being confirmed, but they didn't realize they could never be "unbaptized."

* * *

Mayday! The international distress call was devised in 1923, by Frederick Mockford, a senior radio officer at Croydon Airport in London, who, while searching for an easily understood signal for help, heard French pilots holler "M'aidez! M'aidez!" To Mr. Mockford, the French word for help sounded like "Mayday" in English.

Why not just holler "Help me! Help me!"

* * *

On April 30, while the Russians are polishing their tanks and shining their boots for an impressive parade through Red Square on May 1 to show off their military might, my mother is getting ready to show off her May Basket handiwork. She covers the dining room table with yarn, ribbon, paste, pastel shades of construction paper, and those brass paper fasteners that look like tiny gold mushrooms.

Mother knows how to make three shapes of May Baskets: a plain rectangle, a rolled cone, and the more difficult kind, with four little pointed cups that look like part of an egg carton. She knows how to fill the baskets with popcorn and candy. She knows how to poke and spread the brass fasteners through two ends for a handle. And she knows how to put the baskets in a cardboard box so that they lean against each other and the contents don't spill out.

After breakfast on the big day, confident she has enlisted me in her campaign, my mother leads me to the dining room table and outlines the rest of the maneuver. Holding a cone-shaped basket to demonstrate, she gives me my orders. "You hang the basket on the doorknob and then ring the doorbell and run. Your friend has to run after you, and if he catches you, he has to kiss you."

I'm the only girl in our neighborhood and not keen on being kissed by any of the five boys in our block, but I can run fast and am okay with the plan until Mother says, "And if someone hangs a basket on our front door, you have to run after them, too."

What!? I have to run, catch, and kiss? The popcorn and candy part of the spring custom are okay, but the running and kissing part? Ick. Especially if Peter Edmunds hangs a basket on our door. Peter is older than me, and most of the time he has a runny nose and doesn't use a handkerchief. He just wipes his nose on his sleeve or sticks out his tongue and licks the snot off his upper lip.

And, of course, early on May 1, it's Peter who hops up the porch steps to our front door. My stomach lurches like it does when my father forces me to eat at least one slimy canned green bean. When Peter rings the bell, Mother, whose wide grin spreads across her face, is right there to make sure I follow the rules.

Peter leaps off the porch and begins running around the side of our house toward Mrs. Schindler's flower garden. I let Peter get a good head start. Maybe he will make it all the way through the garden to his home, and I won't have to fulfill the final act of the stupid ritual. But when Peter rounds the corner into Schindler's yard, he looks over his shoulder and sees that I am just on the bottom step of our porch. Peter slows down. I slow down, too. Peter goes even slower and so do I. The few yards between us become a few less. As the distance narrows, I am barely moving my reluctant feet through the grass. The slow and slower motion May Day chase ends when Peter reaches the white wooden trellis that is the entrance to Mrs. Schindler's flowers. He falls down. On purpose. I stand trapped under the arched white arbor.

What if I had known then that I didn't have to kiss Peter?

What if I had known that I didn't even have to play my mother's games.

Not *any* of them.

* * *

Don, my trusted pastor friend, stops me in the narthex after worship. "The Staff Parish Relations Committee voted to give you emerita status," he announces with a big grin.

"Ha. I know what *that* means. Old. Don't meddle. Stay home. Read a book. Make cookies for the bake sale."

Don's face crumples.

Instantly sorry for what I have said, I apologize and say thank-you.

Why does my smart mouth spit venom?

Why can't I receive a gift?

Must be my mother's fault.

* * *

We can be burdened by bad stories.
— Rebecca Solnit

* * *

Mother hangs up the telephone that sits on a small table beneath the agonizing Jesus who is leaning his body over the rock in the Garden of Gethsemane. He is praying that his father will keep him from being killed. I am holding my breath. Waiting to see if my mother will let me go to a party at Judy Redford's house next Tuesday after school.

Mother turns away from the telephone and tells me I can't go to Judy's house. Mother says that Mrs. Redford is forming a Brownie Scout Troop and not all the little girls in second grade were invited, so I can't go.

I don't know what a Brownie Scout Troop is, but my best friend, JoAnn, was invited and she is going, and Susan and Ellen and Patti Jo all got invitations, and they are going and I want to go too.

I want to be in Brownie Scouts.

My mother says no.

My mother says everyone should be invited, just like everyone can come to the Methodist Church every Sunday if they want to. Even if they ride up in a farm wagon pulled by a team of horses and sit in the front row and stink and snore through the service, like Fred and Annie. Or even if she wipes her nose on the bulletin, like Etta, and even if they are deaf, like Dr. Horton, the 10-foot-tall-at-least retired dentist who comes in two syllables late during the unison prayer.

Like an echo.

My mother says everyone can belong at church. But I don't want to go to church. I want to go to Brownie Scouts.

At supper, my father agrees with my mother and leaves for another church meeting. While my mother is ironing my father's dress shirts and listening to *Fibber McGee and Molly*, I cry that my stomach hurts and I want the hot water bottle to take to bed with me and hold against my belly.

My mother says no.

I ask again.

She says no.

When I whine and ask again, she hollers, "Fix it yourself!"

I fix it by obeying a voice that urges me to pour the boiling water down my pajama tops before filling the red rubber skinned pouch.

The blister on my belly the next morning is shaped like the Girl Scout emblem.

* * *

How did I survive 25 years of preaching?

During those years, I hoped the story we played out Sunday after Sunday would free people up instead of reinforce their idolatry, but there was no evidence that the flapping of my lips had any effect. When Bob lost his job, or Heather's father stuck his penis in her 11-year-old vagina, or Ray's wife and two grandchildren were killed in a tangle with a semi, folks didn't want my theology. They wanted my presence. They wanted assurance that God the Father and Jesus Christ his son would fix it.

So I showed up. I couldn't fix it, but maybe my presence was more important than 25 years of sermons.

* * *

The doorbell rings as Rusty and I are settling on her couch, each holding a cup of tea and ready for a long-awaited visit. Jane, Rusty's daughter, appears and says she'll answer the door. Though we hear muffled conversation from the hallway, we continue talking until Jane leads two men into the room.

"These men are detectives from the police department, Mom," she says. "They want to talk with you and Dad."

Rusty nods. The men, both in their late 40s, are dressed in suits, shirts, and ties. No one speaks while Jane finds chairs for the men and leaves to find her father, but while throats are cleared, thumbnails checked, and pants legs straightened, my mind is fidgeting on how this interruption will affect my time with Rusty.

Our 11:00 date had been set a week prior. I left Racine at 8:00, figuring three hours would be plenty of time to allow for road trouble, pit stops, and finding Rusty's new home in Menasha. When nothing impeded my travel and I realized my arrival would be way early, I stopped at Hardee's parking lot in Oshkosh and called to see if an early arrival was okay.

It was. Rusty answered the door and let go of her walker for a familiar and too-long-since-happening hug. We were on the couch and only a few minutes into our visit when the doorbell signaled the break in our reconnecting.

The sticky silence between the detectives, Rusty, and me, is broken as Tom and Jane enter the room. Tom, a tall, stolid man in his late 80s, lowers himself into a recliner that is clearly his. Jane stands behind her father. All of us look at the detectives. And wait.

I'm still holding my breath when one of the detectives looks first at Rusty and then Tom and says, "We need to ask if you are the parents of Peter McKenzie?"

"Yes?"

The detective looks at Tom and says, "We're sorry to tell you that your son was found dead this morning."

"Oh."

Rusty's heavy sigh hangs in the room silent for several moments until Tom and Jane ask where-when-and-how questions. Both detectives, seeming in no hurry to leave, provide information and answer questions gently. Aware of my presence as an outsider in the midst of a fragile intimacy, I do not speak until Jane closes the door behind the departing detectives.

"Shall I leave?" I ask Rusty.

"No." She shakes her head and reaches for my hand. "Stay."

I don't remember much about the rest of the afternoon. I remember Rusty sitting motionless for a while, her back against the couch cushion. I remember the tinges of gray in her short curls. I remember her pushing herself off the couch, taking a few steps over to Tom, kissing his forehead, and then moving slowly to get a drink of water from the kitchenette before joining me back on the couch. I remember looking out the window over Tom's head to see birds flitting around a feeder. I remember Jane facing her mom and sitting on a chair that earlier held one of the detectives.

Over the years, Rusty had shared some of Peter's struggles. None are mentioned this afternoon. Only quiet plans for a service that will acknowledge the gifted man he was.

In the late afternoon, Rusty and I hug goodbye.

* * *

My friends Patti Jo and Susan insist I'm not going to get into heaven because I am not Catholic. One day after school, they sneak me into the back door of St. Joseph's. Through a dusty haze, I spot Jesus in the middle of cream-colored, gold chaos of statues and bric-a-brac.

Horrified, I notice he's been stabbed and his heart, on the outside of his body, is staining his white holy outfit with drips of blood.

Jesus in my church is standing on a rainbow in a stained-glass window. He's stuck, too, but at least he's not bleeding.

I'd like to be with Patti Jo and Susan after I die, but not if Jesus is still bleeding and all those creepy people are hovering around.

* * *

Whoa. Just learned about St. Brigid. Why have I never heard of her? The *Encyclopedia Britannica* places her in recorded history with her death in 525 CE in Kildare, Ireland. However, according to my *Woman's Encyclopedia of Myths and Secrets,* she started out as a Celtic trinity draped in myth.

Back when triune goddesses were worshiped.

When the Catholics arrived and couldn't eradicate the Goddess Brigit's "cult," they canonized her. Well, they canonized *one* of the 19 priestesses from the pagan community active in the area. Evidently *Saint* Brigid quickly fell into line and founded a nunnery. One more usurpation of feminine power.

Whether a goddess or a saint, Brigid could turn water into beer, and once she provided enough beer from one barrel to refresh the parched throats of people in 18 churches. February 1 is her feast day. Of course, she is lower class than Jesus, but Bridget Beer would be a hit in Wisconsin.

* * *

The church is a whore, but she's my mother."
— Overheard at a United Methodist clergy meeting

* * *

The stained-glass window Jesus of my childhood is busy during worship keeping the people he has died for in order. Old Doctor

Horton, the 10-foot-tall-at-least retired dentist I mentioned earlier, who sits in the third pew from the back on the right side of the sanctuary, is deaf. Even though he has a hearing aid dangling from his left ear, he comes in three syllables late during the congregational responses. We all wait for him to catch up.

My best friend, Sarah, and I stifle our giggles.

We also stay away from Fred and Annie, who sit in the very front row only several feet from Reverend Anderson's flapping black robe. They live in a dirt floor shack at the southwest edge of my Grandpa Field's farm and drive into town with a team of horses hitched to a flatbed wagon.

They stink.

Fred must shave once in a while, because he doesn't have a lengthy beard, just stubble. Always stubble. He wears his work pants and a plaid flannel shirt and sometimes snores in his sleep during the sermon. Annie wears a goofy grin. No makeup. Her cut-short black hair is kind of rumply. Like her housedress. Mother, who occasionally takes Fred and Annie a casserole, warns me not to eat the peanut butter and jelly sandwiches that they bring to potlucks.

There are women my father doesn't like: Mona Shachtsneider, who sees everything and whose long nose leads her into it, and Elna Retzlaff, who complains constantly about one or another body ailment. "She's a hypochondriac," my father says. "Her gravestone will read, 'See? I told you I was sick.'"

Mother's nemesis is Mabel Vesley. Mabel doesn't like the color my mother chooses for the tablecloths to use for the Tuesday Rotary Club lunches. She overrides my mother's suggestions for the dessert, and gripes about the onions in the meatloaf.

And, of course, my parents both complain about the preacher. No matter who is occupying the parsonage and pulpit, the man (always a man) has major flaws. His sermons are boring, he doesn't call on the shut-ins enough, and he doesn't fold the bulletins right.

Me? A pastor? Who the hell's idea was that?

* * *

I am walking down the hallway toward the bathroom. I see my mother, Phoebe, sitting on the lid of the toilet. She is in her light blue bathrobe and looks like she did in the last few weeks of her life – bent over, head hanging over her chest.

I am startled. It's just her ghost, I think. She can't harm me. Besides this is a dream.

"No, it isn't," Phoebe says. She gets up off the toilet and starts walking toward me. As she approaches, her head shrinks into the size of a baseball. "Do not put me in a nursing home," she hisses. "Do not put me in a nursing home!" she repeats as her bleached-white naked arms reach for me.

"This isn't a dream! It's real!"

I wake up screaming.

Mother died a year ago in a hospital after a severe stroke. She *never* was put in a nursing home.

What does she want?

* * *

My sister, Margaret, calls.

"Mother is in the hospital," she reports. "She has a perforated ulcer."

"Oh, my. Do I need to drive over?"

"I don't think so. At least not right away. She's okay. She'll be in the hospital a few days."

"Well, can I do something?" I ask. "Like make phone calls?"

"I've pretty much called the folks I think need to know."

"The pastor?"

"She didn't want him called."

"What?!"

"She said I should tell Cinda, that Cinda would tell her mother, and her mother would call the pastor."

"Oh, God!" I scream into the phone. "That's the crap that drove me nuts. I'm still trying to learn to ask directly for what I want."

"I know," my sister says. "Me, too. But she always gets what she wants."

The next day I drive 75 miles to see my hospitalized mother. She tells me Pastor Eric was in her room within four hours of her admittance.

* * *

Mothers are easier to love dead.
— My clergy friend, Judith

* * *

"I want you to look at this," my mother says shortly after I arrive. As she hands me the well-worn blue folder, I know she wants me to go over her funeral plans.

Again.

Mother is 91, so I guess the topic is timely, but she has been talking about dying for 20 years. She wants to be cremated and her ashes planted on top of my father's grave.

Does she realize she'll have the dominant position? For eternity?

"What do you want me to do with this?" I plop onto her well-worn couch and hold her death wishes in my lap.

Mother sits slightly forward on her kitchen chair a few feet away from me in this cramped, subsidized apartment. "I want you to check on my funeral plans," she says. "I had listed Jane as a survivor."

Mother's request reminds me that my aunt died recently. The wife of Uncle Dean, the uncle who taught me to drive the Farmall tractor. Still wondering how my mother allowed me to help with haying when I was nine, I open the folder, and flip through familiar papers and documents until I find a planning guide from Albrecht Funeral Home.

"The only address on this is Milton," I say, holding up the booklet. "Do you know where their Edgerton place is located?"

"Maybe out on the road toward Fulton."

The road toward the tiny town of Fulton is called Main Street. But the "main" street in Edgerton, with all the stores, banks, and restaurants, is named Fulton Street. No wonder I ended up schizophrenic.

"I'll look it up in your phone book."

I get up and move four short steps across the carpet to her desk and find the phone book next to the magnifying machine on loan to her from the Lions Club.

"Albrecht Funeral Homes and Cremation Services is listed on South Main Street," I say. "Have you talked with anyone there recently?"

"No. I guess someone should."

Someone means me. Or maybe my sister or brother. Mother has difficulty asking for what she wants.

Then, remembering that she *did* want me to check her survivor list, I pick up the planning guide again and find the form that will help the funeral home write her obituary. Mother's writing in in her pre-macular-degeneration handwriting, is easy to read. I blot out Aunt Jane's name with my Zebra F-301 ball point.

I don't realize I've pleased my mother until I'm half-way through my 75-mile trip home.

* * *

"What do you want for Christmas, Mother?"

"World peace and my children happy."

Mother can't say what she wants. How many days in the psych unit before I figured out the difference between *want* and *need?*

That it was okay to *want* something?

Without guilt?

That it was okay to want the release form so that I could go for a walk?

That it was okay to want to shave my legs without an aide watching me?

That it was okay to want a roommate who didn't smoke?

* * *

I Google Hannahannah to learn more about her. I read again that theologians regard her as a minor deity. Naturally. But the theologians—probably all male—agreed that when the more important weather god, Taru, disappears, Hannahannah is the one they call on to send out a bee to find him.

A bee? Why a bee? I grab my *Women's Dictionary of Symbols and Sacred Objects.* Look up bee.

OMG!

Bees are hymenoptera, "veil-winged," recalling the hymen or veil that covered the inner shrine of the Goddesses' temple, and the officiating nymph (high priestess) who bore the title of Hymen and ruled over marriage rituals and the honey-moon.

No wonder the male theologians relegate Hannahannah to a lower status than men. Women carry way too much sexual power. They're dangerous.

* * *

Take the name of Jesus with you, child of sorrow and of woe;
it will joy and comfort give you; take it then where'er you go.
— Hymn #536, *The United Methodist Hymnal*
Words: Lydia Baxter, 1870
Music: William H. Doane, 1871

* * *

Jesus is probably feeling betrayed. How can I be looking for another story when Jesus was the one who saved me, pulled me out of the locked darkness in St. Elizabeth's psych unit?

Well, the *name,* Jesus. Just the *word* Jesus.

March 15, 1970

The voices that convinced me to kill myself to prove my love for Father God branded the rules for the dead in my brain. Don't move. Don't talk. Keep your eyes shut. I follow the rules until a sudden flurry of people begin pushing and pulling at my feet and legs and someone slips off my loafer (the other one must still be caught in the banister) and someone else sits me up to reach the buttons on the back of my blouse (the white short-sleeved blouse with embossed designs on front) and someone else peels away my socks and red plaid pants.

I break the rules and open my eyes.

Three attendants are bustling around a too-brightly-lit room. All three are dressed in white. White pants. White shirt. White blouses. White skirts. Each woman is wearing a stiff white hat and a small white plastic nametag pinned over the pocket on the left side of her uniform top. I strain to focus on a name and read *Johanna* in small, square, black print. I struggle to connect frayed wires in my brain.

Johanna. Sounds like Joseph. Joseph and Mary. Joseph and Mary and Jesus. I string Johanna's name onto a necklace of names like beads on a rosary. Johanna-Joseph-Mary-Jesus. The searing light in the room stings my eyes. Jesus-Mary-Joseph-Johanna. I cling to the sacred umbilical cord and float backward through amniotic waters. Backward.

Back into the Great Silence.

I wake in complete darkness. Alone. I am lying on a slab in a cement vault. I do not know where I am. A crypt? I know I am dead. Waiting. I must be in purgatory. A holding tank. Waiting. Waiting.

Blankets of darkness roll over me in suffocating waves. Unanswered questions squeeze like a vise into my temples. What if someone comes who doesn't know the secret way the Jesus story is being played? What if they bring needles and knives and tubes and try to embalm me? What if the blood I need for the next life leaks out onto their stainless steel slab?

Maybe they forgot me. Maybe I won't be able to go anywhere or talk with anyone for years and years and maybe the Catholics are right and a prescribed number of candles have to be lit and prayers said before I will be admitted into heaven.

My legs shake. My stomach lurches with spasms. I can't breathe. I want to call my husband. But if I call him, will the sound of my voice be a summons that will kill him? Is Stan ready to die, too? Maybe *he* is waiting, too. Maybe the rule is *I* have to call someone *I* love so they can die, too. Maybe I have to call my husband before he can die. But what if Stan doesn't want to die? Do I have to kill him? I don't want to kill him. I squeeze my eyes shut. Try to force the right answer. Tears slip down my cheeks and into my ears.

When I open my eyes again, I see a faint square of light coming through a small window a few steps away. I roll off the side of the hard pallet and hurry toward the dim glow. I bump my left arm against something cold and hard. A doorknob! I grab it with both hands and try to turn it. Locked! Trapped. In the dark. Locked in a cell between heaven and hell. Alone!

Then the suffocating panic squeezes a name through the cracks in my memory. Jesus. The name, Jesus. Just the name, but a name that is one of the beads tied to the sacred necklace of names I saw when they took off my clothes. Jesus-Mary-Joseph-Johanna. *Johanna.* I remember her name! Only the name Johanna. As if her name all by itself, like Jesus, is some magic, abracadabra word.

Through a small window that is reinforced with wire woven into hexagonal designs like Grandma Field's chicken coop, I can see a dimly lit, empty hallway. I scream and rattle the doorknob and cry, *"Johanna. Johanna!"* until suddenly two wide-open eyes peek in at me through the threaded wire. Johanna. Johanna, a name fastened to a holy tether that led backward to another name.

Jesus. A name. A word that summoned help.

* * *

Clergy are both priest and prophet. The priest listens to the people and talks with God. The prophet listens to God and talks with the people.
— Bishop David Lawson

* * *

Old Testament prophets, speaking for Yahweh, hoped that the words they spoke went out and then returned having fulfilled what God wanted. Dabar was the Hebrew word for those boomerang proclamations. Prophets dreaded that their words might disappear into a void or return without having completed God's purpose.

What happened to all those words I preached? Having learned my homiletics well, I always included the Good News of God's love, but had no way of knowing if my blathering had any effect. One Sunday I pictured my words spewing from my mouth and plunging to the floor right in front of the pulpit. They didn't even make it to the first row of pews, which most of the time were empty anyway because good church people choose to sit in the back.

And now? What about these words I'm tapping into this 20th century wonder?

On September 30, 2018, I began searching for ways to survive as an old woman in a patriarchal culture. Trump and company are still in charge. I have turned 80. My husband, Charlie, is in a memory care unit and today is Covid-19 Day #125 on my calendar.

I'm still here.

Obviously I've been surviving. Sheltered from visiting, hugging, and eating with others, I've relied on *words*. Not only these words I vomit out into this six-year-old iMac. I've survived by words from

89

my family and friends. Words of comfort, support, love, laughter, wisdom, and, sometimes, important information, like which grocery store has toilet paper.

This computer with my megazillions of words could crash at any moment, fall into a void, and never come back to me.

But I would still have family and friends.

How about the *word* Dabar? Even before I learned its meaning, I figured it wasn't the nearest neighborhood watering hole.

* * *

First Song #4

Little feet be careful
Where you lead me to
Anything for Jesus
I would gladly do.

I wasn't glad to sing. Or play the piano. Or organ. I wasn't doing that shit for Jesus. I was doing it for my father, whom Reverend Thomlinson called Mr. Methodist because my father followed all the rigid rules of the denomination's founder, John Wesley.

Just like Wesley, my father was frugal, anal retentive, didn't drink, smoke, gamble or swear and was at church several times a week. And I learned a couple years ago that my father was unlucky in love.

Just like Wesley.

Twenty years ago, Charlie and I visited John Wesley's house in London and saw his bed, desk, and shoes. Tiny shoes. Size 4 or 5, maybe. Like they'd fit the bound feet of a Chinese woman. Wesley obviously saved his feet by traveling on horseback. My father, whose shoe size was 11, drove Chevrolets and bound *my* feet in that stupid song.

* * *

Occasionally, the pastor chose #184 in the 1939 hymnal.

Make me a captive, Lord, and then I shall be free.

Force me to render up my sword, And I shall conqueror be . . .

At age 11, I didn't get it. I knew Jesus died for me and that I was supposed to follow him and obey all the rules *his* father and *my* father said.

It didn't sound like freedom.

I didn't get it at 30. Hadn't I been successful in dying like Jesus did for his Father? They said they would unlock the door of Room 205 and let me go home to be a good wife and mother, but *only if* I followed Dr. Henning's rules.

Dr. Henning wouldn't let me talk about Jesus or God.

Trapped.

I think I get it now. The church and the psych unit are pretty much the same.

* * *

1986

"Know what you're going to lose," Rusty advises during my phone call to her.

"Oh. Well, we wouldn't have one of those pictures in the newspaper," I laugh. "You know. Couples celebrating their 50th anniversary."

Why did I laugh? And why is that the first thing I think of? As if I've stuck in this marriage just to win some sort of social recognition prize.

Rusty doesn't comment.

"And," I say, adding another future loss, "I wouldn't share in all the money Stan will inherit when his parents die."

Money. Where did that come from? I'm not laughing now. I'm so shallow.

Then I realize that ever since the hospitalizations, my husband has been the one who keeps in contact with our children. For 15 years most of the information about our children—all grown and on their own now—comes from him.

If I go ahead with this divorce, I will lose my children.

* * *

"Stanley doesn't want to pay me half of his pension," I tell Jim-the-priest. "He wants me to come to his office to talk about it."

"Are you entitled to half?"

"Yes, but I'm scared to meet him."

"I'm going to give you advice worth $2,000 of therapy," Jim says. "When you are frightened because you have to face an enemy or difficult situation, there are two ways you can gain a sense of your own power. You can choose your *location* and you can take an *ally*."

"Location?"

"Yes. A place you feel safe."

"I don't feel safe with Stanley *anywhere*, and certainly not in his office. He would be sitting behind his shield of a desk on a mammoth black horse Naugahyde chair with wheels."

"How about inviting him to have a cup of coffee at Big Boy? Or at your friend Rusty's house?"

"Maybe. Big Boy might work. At least we'd be sitting across from each other in a booth. I'd have more equal access to the air in the room. But an ally? You mean like taking another person?"

"Could be, if the person is someone who will advocate for you, like Rusty. But an ally doesn't have to be a person. Just something that you take that reminds you of your own power."

"You mean like a teddy bear?"

"If that works for you. Or you could put a talisman in your pocket, or wear a special piece of clothing. Some people wear crosses, but I know that wouldn't be your choice."

"I thought of another option. A shotgun . . . Hey! I'm just kidding."

"Good."

"So, location, location, location . . ."

". . . And ally."

* * *

Hannahannah. Why do you keep bugging me? You show up while I'm soaping my face in the shower, watching the mergansers on the lake, or trying to rearrange the paper scraps on the kitchen tablecloth to blend in with the striped designs so that I don't have to get up and pick up and clean up one more fucking time.

You obviously aren't a domestic goddess.

The only reason I let you mess with my mind is that you are a *grandmother* goddess. And, at 9,000 years old, you ought to have some tips that would help me manage old age with an out-of-whack heart, a husband with dementia, and a president that Mika Brzezinski calls a runaway beer truck.

To say nothing of 16 grandchildren and seven great-grandchildren.

You sit three feet above me on my file cabinet, your clay eyes looking down as I'm setting little type characters into this electronic gizmo. Have you become acquainted with the figurine next to you? The grieving woman I squeezed out between my locked-up fingers in the psych unit.

Here's a hunk of clay Charlotte-the-occupational-therapist said. Play with it, she said.

How did that ugly ball of dirt turn into that bent over woman, her head down, her arms folded tightly over a hollow stomach?

She never got a name. She never got fired in the therapist's kiln. She is only 43 years old.

And, you, Hannahannah. Surviving nine millennia you must know something to help me.

* * *

Jesus is pissed with me. Maybe because I've been looking for goddesses. Or maybe his daddy is punishing me because for the first time since birth, I'm skipping the Holy Week drama. When Notre Dame went up in flames on Monday of Holy Week, I took it as a sign that God blessed my decision to participate in an online Bending Genres writing workshop.

I was *so* wrong.

Instead of suffering with Jesus through his crucifixion and resurrection, I ended up agonizing at my iMac trying to figure out the right buttons to poke to get in and out of the workshop.

Good Friday morning was good. Up at 5:00, showered, dressed, breakfasted, grocery shopped, chicken in the slow cooker for supper, and lunch for 11:45 all ready to go. Quivering with anticipation, I logged in to the workshop at 11:57 and was immediately confused with all the categories, options, and icons on the dashboard.

I didn't begin to cry until 1:20. Three phone calls to the workshop leaders Meg and Corey before Corey said he couldn't understand why only the dashboard came up when I logged in. He eventually got me to the Welcome to this Workshop page, and while Jesus was busy dying (again), I bled black-and white-impulses into a post. At 7:44 p.m., I poked Group A and clicked on Publish and rewarded myself with a glass of Aldi's $2.89 Cabernet Sauvignon.

April 13. The next morning. Holy Saturday.

While God is performing his (has to be *his*) rabbit-out-of-the-hat trick in the womb tomb, I am back at the Dashboard Posts, eager for a day of iMac prayer. With new confidence, I successfully log in, poke posts, see my title and name, but only a blank page.

No sentences.

No paragraphs.

No story.

I hold back tears and call Corey again. He can't figure out what has happened to my completely gone into-the-ether six hours of work post.

Had I poked Group A? Yes.

Clicked on Publish? Yes.

Saved the draft?

Shit.

Corey's magic fingers somehow retrieve my six hours of work. Before I return to the fickle iMac, I soothe myself by grinding Colectivo Decaf Sumatra beans and waiting five minutes before pushing down the French Press.

No programs to set. No buttons to push. And no tears.

Was I creating "Conversation between the Disciples on Holy Saturday" when Rusty's daughter, Jane, called to tell me her mom died?

Rusty. The woman who sat with me on the closet floor of Room 205 St. E's psych ward and lent me the words to keep the Red Rubber Demon from killing me.

Rusty. The woman who, after I spent yet another weekend in the psych unit, suggested, "Nancy, if you need a break, why don't you go to the Holiday Inn?"

Rusty. The woman who lent me her house for an afternoon of adulterous love while she was at work.

Through choking sobs, I hear Jane invite me to a poetry event in honor of my longtime friend. While I've been trying to find a goddess with a story that will help an old woman—a technologically challenged old woman—to survive in a patriarchal culture, Rusty's daughter calls to tell me her mom is dead.

All on this dark hole womb tomb day.

April 14. Today. Easter. Lilies. Hims–Christ the Lord is Risen Today. Ah-ah-ah-ah-ah-le-ay-lu-oo-yah and, my dear, dead friend, Rusty, shows up as I'm writing.

I get it now.

I've been searching for an old woman goddess and an old woman goddess found me.

* * *

How come Jesus gets 364 days a year to run around telling stories, healing people, and facing down religious authorities, but the goddess gets only one day a year? Only on Holy Saturday, when the guy is dead dead dead and sealed in the tomb, the goddess is free to move into our lives unimpeded.

One day? Only one day? It isn't fair.

Jesus even gets February 29.

Thank some god or other that Rusty found me yesterday.

* * *

In the dream, I watch a depressed, sunken in woman leave her female partner and risk asking a man to dance. Shortly after they begin to dance, she quickly pulls away and hurries back to a place at the room's wall. He follows. She spills out her anguish to him. When they hug goodbye, she is healed.

I long to be whole and happy again and want healing, too. Now the man sits next to me. Neither of us speaks and he gets up to leave. Disappointed that he is leaving, I remember a 3:00 appointment we had. Now it is 5:00. I was so engrossed in watching him heal the other woman, I forgot the appointment. He leaves without reminding me.

What the hell does this dream mean?

"Follow the dream 'I,'" suggested one therapist. "See what your ego is doing." Does this have anything to do with Charlie? Am I not asking verbally for what I want?

My mother's best legacy.

* * *

July 30, 2019

Today is Charlie's 83rd birthday. Who knows why I scanned the ages of the deceased in the *Racine Journal Times* obituaries.

Or why I read the whole column describing the life of Wilma Bettenhausen.

With the exception of her early work history, Wilma's obituary could be mine.

She was the first born of Christian parents, graduated from high school with honors, and studied piano for 10 years. She was "a loving wife and mother of four children" and especially enjoyed canning, cooking, baking, and sewing. She was active at her church, soloist in the choir, member of the women's group, and a Sunday School teacher. *She wrote poetry, and a couple of years before she died, she fulfilled her lifelong goal of publishing a book of her poems.* (emphasis mine)

Someone summarized 97 years of Wilma's life in a 12-inch newspaper column, but I wonder what that someone didn't write. Did she scream at her sons when she discovered the BB gun holes in the plastic cover of her new Singer sewing machine. Did she fall in love with her choir director, get really good at feigning orgasms, pour boiling water over her wrists?

And, did some sadistic housewife give her a set of Revere Ware for a wedding gift? Copper bottoms that she had to clean *every time* she used one of those fucking pans? *Every day* for the last 61 years of her life?

Do I have time to publish a book of poetry before I die?

* * *

October 2019

A goddess named Bonnie shows up this morning promptly at 8:30. Slightly shorter than me and a little chunkier, she is wearing jeans and a purple tee-shirt with *Home Instead* printed in small white letters on the upper left side of the shirt. She introduces herself to Charlie and me, and listens as I describe activities he likes. She nods when I open the refrigerator to show her options for lunch. Soup. Tuna salad sandwiches.

She'll help Charlie put the 500-piece alphabet puzzle together.

She'll keep him from setting another fire.

Fifteen minutes later, I am in the Honda Accord and not even out of the driveway when all the Bonnies I have known hop in the car with me.

Bonnie, my neighbor, who is already in Arizona for the winter.

Bonnie, whose husband and I share the same birth date.

Bonnie, whose uterus was filled with fibroids.

Bonnie Staffen, whose daddy brought a Chinese hat back from the war and Bonnie brought it to kindergarten for show-and-tell and when Bonnie, Gentry Drake and I finished our cutting and pasting the polar bears and iceberg onto the blue construction paper and Bonnie grabbed her Chinese hat and Gentry and I began chasing after her to try to get it because we wanted to try it on and I got grabbed by Miss Monteith and spanked and my daddy told me if I ever got spanked in kindergarten, he'd give it to me twice as hard at home.

And, of course, "My Bonnie Lies Over the Ocean," who, according to Google, wasn't a beautiful woman at all but a folk song about Bonnie Prince Charlie, who was defeated at the Battle of Culloden in 1746, escaped to France, and died in Rome, a "drink-befuddled and bitter old man."

But this morning, while I am driving the Bonnies and me on my necessary six hours away for mental health, the Goddess named Bonnie from Home Instead will keep the handsome and befuddled Bauer-King Charlie from starting another fire.

99

* * *

This morning, when I saw the linen-covered communion elements on the altar, I remembered Rusty's years-ago advice: "You can't say 'yes' until you can say 'no.'" I decided to try out the *no* and sat solid in the pew while Charlie struggled to get over my legs so he could join the sacred string of people who dipped and sipped.

Laura, sitting behind me, and back from swallowing the ritual, poked my shoulder and whispered, "Should I flag someone down and have them bring communion to you?"

I turned, shook my head, and mouthed thank you.

Five minutes later, after the closing hymn and the benediction, I left the sanctuary. Nothing happened. No lightning struck. No guilt.

No.

No.

No.

Will I ever get to 'yes' with Jesus? Jes-yes? What would a free and honest *yes to Jesus* look like?

* * *

"This is my body given for you. This is my blood shed for you." In my dream, fresh blood is seeping into the edge of a piece of white bread torn into a hunk the size of my fist. Was the dream because I didn't take communion yesterday?

Is Jesus even in my unconscious, insisting I suck up his words?

At Mocha Lisa, I try to swallow the pulsing dream image whole with my skim milk latte. Without choking.

* * *

Maybe we weren't at the Last Supper,
but we're certainly going to be at the next one.
— Bella Abzug

* * *

Because Murdock claims excavation is necessary, I keep digging back through layers of matriarchal ancestors, like an archeologist sifting through names and ashes of stories.

Was my mother named Phoebe after her great-grandmother? Did her mother, who named her, also know about the biblical Phoebe, a wealthy benefactor and leader in the early Christian church?

The Apostle Paul entrusted the Phoebe he knew to carry a letter to the Christians in Rome and included her name as a necessary introduction so the church officials (male) would know that the woman presenting the papyrus wasn't an imposter.

The name Phoebe showed up in the Bible only that *once*.

My mother's name showed up too many times to count during the 70 years she was a member of the Edgerton Methodist church.

She was the only Phoebe.

She taught Sunday School, was financial secretary, was officer in the women's group, sang in the choir, stitched banners, created program booklets, and was in church several times during the week doing the odd jobs that the pastor du jour requested.

But unlike her wealthy biblical namesake, Mother was poor. Widowed at 55, she lived alone in a subsidized apartment on Social Security and died at 93, leaving $18,000, a box of greeting cards, and a few pieces of furniture, including a TV that Fred down the hallway came and took away.

She also left a phalanx of women who lived in her building and stopped in daily. One put drops in her eyes. Another a patch on her hip. One distributed her pills. One reached things from the top shelf of her cupboard. Another fetched her mail. Another looked up an address on a computer.

They all loved her.

They put on their small-town sniffing looks of disgust when my siblings and I scheduled a meal *before* our mother's funeral instead of after.

The biblical Phoebe lives in perpetuity. My mother lives in the stories told about her. Stories about my Great-Great-Grandmother Phoebe are non-existent.

Why am I writing about my female ancestors if the stories only live about five generations?

* * *

My grandmother, Bessie Azelia Craig Addie Field Sellnow, wanted one of her grandchildren to name a kid Chadwick—her mother's maiden name. Grandma remembered a man stopping at her grandparents' door with information about a castle in Scotland owned by some Chadwick ancestor. The castle could be Ezra Chadwick's if he could find a document with the correct coat of arms.

Sounded like a 19th century scam to me. But what if my great-great-grandfather *had* found said document with the proper provenance? Would I have stuck a name like Chadwick on a little kid? The only Chadwick I knew had thick glasses, a snotty nose, and walked in a stumble with his mouth agape.

Grandma also wanted her children, her grandchildren, her great-grandchildren, and assorted spouses *all* to be together at least once for a summer picnic in Milton Park.

Grandma died, disappointed, at 69 years old. No Chadwick castle. No grandchild named Chadwick. No family picnic with all the descendants. But Grandma lives on through the woes she wove into my childhood: miscarriages, son's drowning, house fire, widowed three times.

* * *

My mother said, "You can't wear pink and red together."

My mother's mother said, "You can't wear anklets because the gypsies will steal you."

My mother's mother's mother said, "You can't give the baby away."

My mother's mother's mother's mother said, "You can't marry a Catholic."

All my mothers said, "You can't air your dirty linens in public."

Metaphorically deprived as a young wife, I thought that meant I couldn't hang bloodstained bedsheets on the clothesline.

* * *

"The date has been set," I tell Rusty, over lunch at the Casbah.

"Have you decided about your name?"

"No. I don't want to be Nancy Ore. Twenty-nine years is long enough. And sometimes when I introduce myself, I often hear a crappy '*or* what?'"

"What about your maiden name?"

"I've thought about it, but I've been Nancy Ore 11 years longer than Nancy Bauer, and I don't want the hassle of changing everything. You know. All the forms. Papers. I don't know what name to go with, but I still have a few weeks to decide."

"Is there a rush? Couldn't you decide after the divorce?"

"Yes. I guess so. But I think the day in court is the only shot I get at changing it without being charged."

"Oh. Do you have other options? Names, I mean."

"Ha. Not Schachtsneider or VandenEvenhoven. Maybe I'll just change my last name to Nancy. You know. Nancy Nancy. Fits my split personality."

Rusty grins. We finish lunch. In two days, Rusty will be leaving for the cottage on Dickey's Cay in the Bahamas. When we hug goodbye, I wish her safe travel.

A few days later I get a post card addressed to Nancy Nancy.

* * *

Today Facebook claimed my ex-husband wanted to be my friend.

Now? *Now* he wants to be my friend? He barely talked during the 29 years we were married.

And he's been *dead* for over a year.

My daughter, the one he abused, said he was cremated and his ashes were spread all over one of his favorite spots in Door County.

How on earth could he communicate with me now?

Until he says he is sorry, there is no way in hell I will even consider being his friend.

* * *

How many times has Don, my pastor friend, heard me whine about the male-only godhead? "Check out the Black Madonna," he advises, trying to help my search for a feminine presence in the heavenly panoply.

Black Madonna? I know how important it is to identify with one's spiritual image and am curious to discover a goddess that may be a go-to for my African American friends. Who knew what I would uncover.

"Did you know there is more than one Black Madonna?" I ask Don several days later. "And I am surprised that one of her is ensconced in a chapel in Bavaria."

"Oh?"

"I've been there. I saw her."

People are waving American flags as our bus pulls into the schoolyard. Instead of celebrating the bicentennial in the states, Stan, my then-spouse, and I are on a bus with 17 Appleton East high school students on an exchange trip to Altotting, a small Bavarian town. For the three-week duration of our visit, each of the students stays with a family. Stan and I are housed in the convent, take our meals with the priest of this all-girl's school, and accompany field trips to Salzburg, Hitler's Eagle's Nest, and every home brewery within a 20-mile radius.

On an unscheduled afternoon, Mother Agnes suggests we visit the Shrine of our Lady of Altotting, a site of pilgrimage since 1489, when a three-year-old boy who had drowned was carried by his mother, laid down in front of the Madonna, and began to breathe again.

Stan and I walk to the center of the town and enter another foreign world. Every wall is covered with pictures and small tin or wax figures, brought by people who hope for healing. Surrounded with vivid depictions of bloody body parts, I barely glance at the Black Madonna, a figure about two feet tall and holding the Christ child. The statue is covered in jewels and eclipsed by glitzy surroundings and candles.

Dizzy from sparkle, I am moving toward the door when I see an urn that is purported to hold the heart of King Ludwig II, the crazy king who built Neuschwanstein. I quickly stumble out of the house of horrors.

I report my Black Madonna research to my friend, Don. "There are hundreds. Some out of wood, some of stone. Some black because of original coloring, other others black because of years of candle smoke. But black or white or green," I add, "she is still Mary and only important because of her son. And he's still a male, isn't he?"

* * *

Last night, while I was finishing *Midsummer Murder* in the living room, Charlie stripped the bed. I find the sheets, blankets, bedspread, and pillow cases all carefully folded and stacked against the closet door and my memory-challenged husband sitting on the edge of the mattress dressed in *my* slacks.

"What are you *doing?*" I scream.

"I'm getting stuff ready."

"For *what?*"

"For when they come."

"*Who? Who's coming?*"

He thinks we are moving. That we're not in our own home. That the movers will help us get our *stuff* to the place we're supposed to be living.

I wish I hadn't screamed.

* * *

The bus pulls up to another stop on this Holy Land Tour. How many days have I been living out of my suitcase? Kibitzing in the back of the bus with my cynical friends, Jim and Kathy? Dragging myself off to every sacred site?

Sometimes the bishop's wife stays in her seat and catches a nap, but her husband is leading this tour especially for pastors like me in their first appointment, so I feel a huge *should* at each biblical wonder.

"We have arrived at Mary's Well," Bishop Lawson says, standing in the aisle of the bus and facing his baby pastors. "This is the location of the Annunciation."

"*One* of the locations," Jim whispers and rolls his eyes. "There's another."

Of course there is another. There are two traditional birth sites, two traditional burial sites, why not two holy orgasm sites?

"We'll be here about half an hour," the bishop instructs. "Follow me along the path and down a few steps to the well."

Several people seem eager to see the place the Archangel Gabriel told Mary she was chosen to bear God's son. The Bible says she was initially perplexed at a holy pregnancy but easily acquiesced to her servant role.

Wouldn't she at least want to think about it? Or ask questions like *how* and *when* is this going to happen? And what should she wear?

Maybe before she married Joseph and was relegated to household drudgery, she had planned a girl's getaway on the Mediterranean. Or she could have said, "Why me? Look at my nose. No kid of God's would want to go through life with this proboscis."

I guess one doesn't argue with an angel, and Mary spent the rest of her life running, pondering, and grieving.

Lucky girl.

And now thousands of looky-loos trek thousands of miles to stand at the very place of conception. One *traditional* very place.

Along with my colleagues, I follow the bishop single file to the end of the dirt path and see a trickle of water lit by a few pendant lamps that hover over the sacred site from the top of an arched structure.

Other pilgrims seem genuinely moved. Some are praying, heads bowed. One is wiping tears off her cheeks. I close my eyes and stand in silence, trying to look as if I'm having a moment of spiritual bliss. But the moment warns me that I'm on sacred stuff overload.

The first devotee up the steps and across the path, I find a picnic table, straddle the wooden seat, and wait for the bus. A couple minutes later, Jim-the-cynic approaches. As he joins me at the table, he says, "Well, whaddaya think about that?"

"I think I'm pregnant," I answer.

* * *

Jack Paar is chatting with Phyllis Diller on the new RCA. My boyfriend, Ronnie, and I are in a clutch on the old rose-colored couch. My hands are pressed on a lump beneath his zipper. His fingers are fiddling inside my underpants. Then a weird but pleasant fluttering shivers through me. Confused, I twist away. I'm not interested in kissing Ronnie anymore. At least *that* night.

* * *

My longtime friend Helen died four years ago. I miss her. She had a good mother. A mother who, when talking about body eliminations, said, "Anything that comes out of you is good."

Helen would never have said the word shit.

She didn't criticize my irreverent skepticism about the Virgin Mary. She gave me a wooden triptych painted shiny black with two doors decorated with curlicues of gold and ivory leaves like a DNA helix; the doors open to reveal an icon of Mary and the baby Jesus. The baby Jesus looks about eight years old and stands at his mother's side with two fingers extended from his right hand. Two angels, each holding a staff and some kind of translucent round thing that looks like a fortune teller's globe, are depicted on the inside of the triptych's doors. Although all the figures have halos, they all are morose, as if the crystal ball had already clued them into the baby's future.

Helen was 85 when she died. She was more like a goddess to me than Mary ever was.

So much for Jesus' mom in my life. I keep trying to figure out what to do with Jesus.

* * *

femailcreations.com is offering a Christ Story Bracelet. For only $19.99 (plus shipping), I can have a clear plastic, three-dimensional cross fastened to a "silver-toned" bracelet. Twenty-one tiny colored stones fill the cross, each stone representing a step in the story of Jesus. The description of this piece of jewelry reads, "Wear it and remember the road he walked for your sins."

Do people *really* buy stuff like this? What are they hoping for?

I don't need to spend $19.99 (plus shipping) to be reminded of all those stories. I'm still burdened with the blatant colored spin of sin.

* * *

It's raining Friday after classes, and I'm waiting with my steady boyfriend for his school bus. My new, red-soled saddle shoes (with the white dots in a black strip on the back, like the popular girls are *supposed* to wear) are getting wet. Drops are beading up on the ribs of my boyfriend's dark blue corduroy Future Farmers of America jacket. As his bus appears, a low stirring prompts my embarrassed and shameless whisper, "Are you going to get a rubber?"

He nods.

My stained soul? Like my shoes. Black and white and red all over.

* * *

Gwyneth Paltrow's line of products, goop, is advertising "This Smells Like My Vagina," a scented candle, priced at $75. There is no way I would spend $75 for a candle that smells like Gwyneth Paltrow's vagina.

But how does she know what her vagina smells like?

I *would* spend 10 times the cost of that candle to have Paltrow's flexibility.

* * *

Just when I decide I'm going to quit looking for goddesses, a friend says, "Have you included Kapo, the goddess with a flying vagina?"

"*What*? No! Who is *she*?"

Because my friend's question comes at the end of our Zoom meeting, she doesn't have time to respond. I click the red Leave button and quickly Google "goddess with a flying vagina."

And there she is—Kapo—a Hawaiian goddess of sorcery, described in dozens of references.

Kapo's special power is her ability to detach her vagina and send it wherever she wants. Although I don't learn how she unfastens her vagina, (snaps? zipper? Velcro?), one story is paramount. She hears the cry of her sister, Pele, the goddess of volcanoes, who is being raped by Kamapuaa, half man-half pig. Kapo detaches her Kohe lele and whips it toward the assault. Kamapuaa, excited at seeing a magic vagina, drops Pele to chase after the enticing projectile.

Kapo lands her vagina on the hard surface of a mountain, and the tumescent Kamapuaa smashes into it. Instead of an exotic rapture, he experiences an explosive rupture.

Why was I 80 years old before I heard about Kapo or even considered that my vagina might have had some kind of power? Now Gwyneth Paltrow gets rich by selling the scent of her vagina. Imagine. A vaginal smell detached and dispatched for anyone who wants to squander $75.

Of course, there is the Virgin Mary whose vagina not only was securely fastened but was completely unnecessary. We're not even told if the baby Jesus passed through the tunnel of love on his way to saving the world.

* * *

"The Soothsayer of Solo Sex" is an article on the front page of today's *New York Times* Thursday Styles section. Evidently for years,

Ms. Betty Dodson has coached women how to tone their pelvic floor to enhance masturbation. Gwyneth Paltrow (the woman who knows what her vagina smells like) is one of her students.

Toning my pelvic floor? Until after the birth of my first child, I was too frightened to even look at the pulsing mystery between my legs. And Kegels never worked.

Masturbation? Now I'm more interested to know if Dodson can train me to get to the toilet on time.

* * *

Bessie Azelia Craig Addie Field Sellnow had one-two-three husbands and was responsible for at least 25 percent of the fortune I've spent on psychiatrists, counselors, and spiritual guides.

Grandma Field, a stout woman, filled doorways, including the front door of 707 Blaine Street the day my baby brother was brought home from the hospital. She called me in from playing with Jerry Ratzlaff and gave me one of her favorite commands: "You'll need to take care of your mother, Nancy Lu."

Grandma wasn't specific. So when Mother got asthma and was ferried along with my father and Baby Butch to live with Grandpa and Grandma Bauer for a couple of months, and I had to go to the farm with Grandpa and Grandma Field, I knew I had failed in my responsibility.

A farm wife, Grandma corseted herself each day into a housedress that she covered with an apron she had made out of feed sacks. She had false teeth, the edges of which were tinged in a light green color, as if she'd been chewing on wet grass. She had a mole on the left side of her nose that moved up and down when she ate.

Grandma worked hard. She wiped the sweat off her face with the edge of her apron, moaned with arthritic knees, and put a few gooseberries in her pies for "a little tart," which townspeople might have called her when she became pregnant at 15.

Her lover, Lawrence Addie, also 15, was banished to Kansas to pick strawberries on his cousin's farm. He came home, turned 18, and married Grandma two days later, on her 18th birthday, thereby giving his illegitimate son a father and, within a year, a sister—my mother.

At 20 years old, Lawrence was killed in a tussle with a team of horses and a wagonload of coal. One house fire and one miscarriage later, Grandma married a tenant farmer, Pearl Judson Field, whose wife had died giving birth to twin boys.

Before she died, Grandma buried three husbands and a son.

On my last visit to her, she rolled her head back and forth on the hospital pillow, her hair spread out in twitching strands, like an angry Medusa.

* * *

"I'm counting on you to help me, Hannahannah. I want to hear about your six months underground."

"Why?"

"Well, I'm reminded of my psychotic break and wonder if it's comparable?"

"Tell me about it."

"After a religious seminar, when I realized the whole Jesus thing was a story, I got caught in the plot and thought I had to die to prove my love for a *Father* God. My suicide attempts were weak and unsuccessful, but during my struggle, I split and dropped into a deep maw and then there was a bone-jarring crash of lightning and I was sizzled into a born-again life. Like a man being shot out of a cannon."

Hannahannah replied, "You dropped into the abyss only *once* because you *snapped*? I *choose* to go underground, and I *choose* to return above ground. I do not get ejected or kidnapped like Persephone and some other goddesses that came millennia later than me.

"But I thought you take your time outs because you are angry."

"Yes? So what?"

"A huge cause of my *cracking* was blocked anger. I spent weeks in the hospital unpacking rage. Mostly toward my father."

"Well, there's another difference. I am not trying to please any *male* god."

I said, "That's exactly the reason I've dragged you out of antiquity. I want you to help me survive my old age in a patriarchal world."

"Did you realize you used a male metaphor to describe being thrust into a born-again above ground life?

"You mean like a man being shot out of a cannon?"

"Yes. Does a *woman* ever get shot out of a cannon?"

"I've never heard of one. Why?"

Hannahannah. "How about being shot out of a *canon*? You know. The authoritative biblical texts."

"Oh. A homophone. I love it."

"Yes. Canon. Well?"

"Women don't appear much in canons."

"So they must have been ejected sometime by someone."

"Is *this* the kind of help you are going to give me?"

* * *

114

What am I writing about anyway? Finding a goddess who will help me survive my 80s in a patriarchal culture that is whacking back on women's reproductive rights? Not that I'm hoping to get pregnant, God (some god or other) forbid. If that biblical god tried the Sarah-Hannah-Mary trick on me, I would have to hunt for a doctor willing to be jailed.

Or a bent clothes hanger.

Why am I flailing around every morning at this wireless keyboard that runs out of juice and then I have to figure out which tiny slot I can barely see to plug into a slightly bigger slot in the back of the screen that lets me know when I'm making a speeling mistake (like I just did) with a red line?

I'm becoming afraid this whole thing is about my mother. Phoebe Emogene Addie Bauer, who did the best she could, I guess, with her mothering of me. Which I've complained about and have a file drawer full of stories about how she screwed up my life.

But she *was* spectacular at doing old.

* * *

Oh no. My mother pops up as a woman who did "old" really well. Is she trying to help me? Is this whole search for a goddess who will help me survive being an old woman in a patriarchal culture really about my relationship with my mother?

Shit.

* * *

"What do you want for your birthday?" I ask Mother in my latest phone conversation with her. She will be 80 years old on February 15.

Mother answers with her *every* birthday *every* Christmas answer. "I want world peace and my children happy."

I sigh and pour myself a glass of Two-Buck Chuck.

Anticipating Mother's birthday, my brother, sister, and I have talked about having an open house for her in the subsidized housing facility she has lived in for almost 20 years. The building has a large community room with a completely furnished kitchen that Mother has reserved numerous times for family gatherings.

The spot is perfect for an open house.

Although we have no idea how many people would attend a celebration, Mother has been active in the small town's school, hospital, and church for over 50 years, and everyone who knows her "just loves her."

But none of them has to deal with her like me—her oldest child.

"Reaching 80 is an important milestone," I say. "How about an open house?"

"No! I don't want an open house!" Mother's response is immediate and adamant.

"Really?" Mother has difficulty saying what she wants. I'm surprised at her vehemence about what she *doesn't* want.

"Well, you know how those things are."

"No . . . ?"

And Mother launches into "how those things are." She knows someone named Evelyn, who had an open house, and some long-lost cousin of Evelyn's showed up unexpectedly and they hadn't seen each other for over 30 years and the missing-in-action cousin dominated the whole party because she came and sat down next to Evelyn for over an hour and kept other well-wishers from wishing Evelyn well.

"Oh," I say. I stop myself from pointing out that if that happened to Mother, she could interrupt the wordy windbag. Mother doesn't have enough self-esteem or courage to assert herself.

Except with me.

I reach for the wine bottle.

Into the silence, Mother continues her no-open-house reasons.

"It's unfortunate I was born in February," she says, "because the weather is so unpredictable. You kids would spend a lot of time on decorations, and maybe you would hire caterers, and then there would be a major snowstorm and you'd just end up throwing all that good food down the drain.

"And, there is not enough parking space here," she adds. "There are only three spots for visitors."

I do not remind her of several blocks of available street parking. She would argue on behalf of all the "old people" who couldn't walk that far.

As if she has not convinced me that an open house is a terrible idea, she has one more weapon in her arsenal of refusal.

"Margaret would make Adam and Erik be there," she says, "and Adam and Erik wouldn't want to be there. I can't do that to my grandsons."

"Okay, okay," I say. "No open house."

My capitulation finishes our conversation.

After I hang up, scream, and pour another glass of wine, I call my sister.

Margaret listens, then says, "That sounds just like what she does to me, too. Why do you let it get to you?"

"I don't know," I whine. "I can never do anything that pleases her. Why do I keep trying?"

"The open house idea is a lose-lose situation," Margaret says. "If we have one, she'll be quietly peeved, but if we don't have a party for her, and her friends ask why her *children* didn't give her a big celebration, she'll say ... "

In concert, my sister and I croon Mother's oft-repeated comment ... "Oh, my kids are so busy. I just didn't want to put them out any further."

* * *

If a story comes to you and you don't tell it, it's murder.
— Elie Wiesel

* * *

Several clergy are sitting in a circle listening to a counselor speak about family constellations. The counselor, who says he wants to be called Greg, spends a half hour presenting basic theory and illustrating with a few examples. After answering a couple of questions, he asks the group for a volunteer. His request sucks the air out of the room. No one moves. No one responds. Greg stands motionless in the middle of the circle with his arms at his side, waiting.

Into a frozen silence. Waiting.

Shall I? Most of these colleagues already know my history. Already know I'm certifiably nuts. What have I got to lose?

I raise my hand. Greg unbuttons his suit coat, moves to my chair, and, standing above me, asks, "What family issue would you like to explore?"

Hmm ... my hospitalizations? ... the divorce? ... my daughter? Ah ...

"I feel estranged from Lynn, my oldest child."

"Can you tell me a little about your relationship with Lynn?"

Within seconds, I'm into it. Her letter to me six months after the divorce. Her close relationship with her father. My bad mother guilt.

"How close are you to your mother?" Greg asks, interrupting my self-deprecating mantra.

My mother? What's my mother got to do with this?

"Not very," I admit. "My mother is 75. Widow for 20 years. She lives an hour-and-a-half away. I call every few weeks. Drive over once in a while." I grimace and add, "An hour or two visit is enough."

Greg raises his eyebrows but doesn't pursue my relationship with my mother. Rather, he asks, "What about your mother's relationship with *her* mother?"

From the back seat of the '46 Chev, I see my mother and grandmother on her front porch, still talking while my father is waiting with his hands on the steering wheel and my brother is fidgeting with the window knob.

"Close," I answer.

"And your grandmother's mother?" Greg asks.

How would I know? She was dead before I was born.

I shrug my shoulders. "I don't know. I don't know much about her. Other than she got pregnant when she was 15. The baby was my grandmother."

Greg nods, lifts his left hand to smooth the furrows in his brow, and says, "Okay, I'd like to try something with you. Will you step over here with me?"

Within minutes, I'm at the edge of the circle of colleagues and facing three women whom Greg has chosen from the group. Each one is standing directly behind the other and looking at me.

"This is your mother, grandmother, and great-grandmother," Greg says, pointing at and naming each stand-in. "As you face them, is there anything you want to say?"

119

Look at their faces. This woman is supposed to be my mother. My mother.

Oh. I can't do this. Scared. I don't want to cry.

Sifting quickly through mental memories of abuse, I turn to Greg. "She was physically and emotionally intrusive," I say.

"Don't tell me," Greg says and points toward my three stand-in ancestors. "Tell your mother."

My mother? I see her in her buttoned-up housedress towering over me . . . pulling my brown corduroy pants down . . . forcing me over the edge of the tub . . .

"I . . . can't . . . I don't . . .

Greg nods. "You can," he says softly as if he understands. "You have something to tell her."

My make-believe mother's face is expressionless. I take a deep breath, look directly into her eyes, and let loose stifled anger. "I don't understand why you forced me over the tub to show Tommy's mother my worms . . . why you made me walk to school with Harriet Thorson . . . play with David Owens . . . why you wouldn't let me join the Brownies . . . enter the eighth grade spelling bee . . .

As my list of woes slows down, I notice my anger is diffusing and settling into sadness.

Now what? I can't think of anything else to say.

Then, into my depleted silence, the woman playing my mother says, "I did the best I could at the time."

My mother did the best she could at the time? Her mother and her mother's mother did the best they could at the time? And, me? My daughter? Did I do the best I could at the time?

What does Greg see on my face? He reaches toward me, takes my arm, says thank you, and escorts me back to my chair.

My mother did the best she could at the time.

I don't understand how those few words took up permanent residence in my memory. I don't understand how it echoes, loosens knots of anger, and assuages scars of guilt. I don't understand how the words transform scenes of *my* screaming at my children. I don't understand how I see the scenes in a softer light, a sad, but no longer damning light.

* * *

Because her mother and stepfather were tenant farmers, my mother, Phoebe Emogene Addie, grew up on several small dairy farms in southcentral Wisconsin. She excelled in school and won prizes for her work, but her high school graduation gift from her parents—a nail file—clearly indicated there was no money for college, and Phoebe went to work as a bookkeeper at Milton Power and Light.

At 20, she used her earnings to buy a new 1936 Chevy, which she also shared with her parents. In 1938, she gave Russell Bauer rides to and from Epworth League, a Methodist Episcopal young adult organization.

She married him a year later and handed the steering wheel over to him.

* * *

A visiting bible scholar is lecturing about God at a seminary chapel service. "We don't understand the mystery of the universe," he says. "We stand under it."

Stand under? Stand *under* feels like the missionary position. I don't want to stand under. I want to stand *with* the mystery of the universe. Or more to the point, the way things are going these days: Trump still president; The United Methodist Church "Un-Tied;" my husband, Charlie, sinking deeper into vascular dementia, I want to *with-stand.*

Stand with *what*?

* * *

She tried to comfort me the first time around midnight. I'm twisting in the covers, upset because of the Women in Crisis class.

Dr. Reuther, the prof of the three-credit seminary elective, said the film, interviews with women who had been raped, would help inform our understanding of various kinds of sexual assault. The class—19 women and one man—became immediately engrossed in the film, and the air hung rigid in the room as the women described their experiences. Stranger rape. Date rape. Spousal rape.

I realized my breathing was shallow when the student two chairs in front of me jumped up and shouted, "That's enough! We're being raped again!" She strode quickly behind the 16mm camera and yanked out the plug. "You're all voyeurs," she cried. "We can't stand anymore of this." She grabbed her notebook, rushed out of the classroom, and slammed the door behind her, the departure cracking the spell of the film.

Dr. Reuther dismissed class, but I couldn't dismiss the woman in the film, who through tears, described her husband's behavior.

Spousal *rape*? I'd never heard of spousal rape. Sex between husband and wife couldn't be rape. Could it? Wasn't the wife supposed to submit? Please her husband? I'd never considered he'd *raped* me.

All afternoon and into the evening, the searing scene from the first year of my marriage replayed in an incessant loop.

At midnight, I'm crying and writhing back and forth in the bed when a presence fills the dark room. A presence like the one I floated in during my suicide attempt. Then, I was in oblivion. Alone. Now, the presence is calming and soothing—definitely feminine. She doesn't show her face. She hovers.

I wipe my eyes and sink into a soft velvet envelope of sleep.

The goddess shows me one of her faces a year later. I'm standing in my gold chaplain's jacket on the sixth floor of St. Luke's Hospital in Milwaukee waiting for the elevator. The woman whose room I've just left wouldn't talk about her suicide attempt. She sat on the edge of her bed, picking at the edge of her hospital gown, and answered my questions with a quiet yes or no.

When the elevator door opens, a nurse pushing an old woman in a wheelchair emerges. The elderly woman's eyes are squeezed shut. Her lips are locked into a tight slit, blocking raw cries of pain.

Surprisingly, the goddess appears in the face of that old woman. A face with eyes and nose, but no mouth at all. A face framed with a flowing blue head covering, like the virgin Mary. But a goddess who can't speak. A goddess who can't scream or cry or curse her pain.

Like the woman in the wheelchair.

Like the suicidal woman in room 617.

Like me.

She appears full-bodied after my ordination. I am in a French Town Restaurant booth with a cup of coffee and a banana nut muffin. Home from my grandson's funeral in San Diego, I'm trying to write a sermon. Spread out on the table are the New Revised Standard Version Bible, a commentary on Matthew and a notepad.

An empty notepad. My job: have a sermon on Sunday that will bring Good News of God's love from Matthew's world to the world of the folks sitting in worship. But in my world, my grandson is dead and my daughter is 2,000 miles away.

Nothing in Matthew sparks my creativity. Nothing.

That's when the goddess slips into the booth across from me. This time she has a mouth and a body. A weirdly dressed body. Garish makeup. Dangly earrings. A purple sweatshirt with letters W.O.W. in rhinestones spread across the front.

"I heard you were having trouble with your sermon," she says.

"Uh huh."

"What's the problem?"

"Well . . . "

I don't ask where she came from or how she knew about my difficulty. I just talk. She listens. And, somewhere in our conversation, the scripture comes alive, and at the very moment I gain insight for the sermon, those rhinestone initials shimmer and flash. WOW!

* * *

Recipe for Cockaigne Wheat Bread

Cockaigne: from Old French quoquaigne – *an imaginary land of delicacies*

Heat 2 cups of milk to 115 degrees. Pour over one cup old-fashioned oatmeal in large bowl. Cool to lukewarm.

Forget Ole's black-and-white drugstore and the three men on shadowy stools.

Add 4½ ounces yeast to ¼ cup lukewarm water. Add to oatmeal and milk.

Forget your great-grandpa's hand when he gives you the strawberry ice cream cone.

Mix in ¼ cup oil, ½ cup, wheat bran, 2 lightly beaten eggs, 2 tsp. salt, 2 cups wheat flour, 4 cups bread flour.

Forget the park, the long walk home through the towering trees, hanging on to your Great Grandpa's other hand. The missing fingers. The railroad accident.

Knead and knead until your fingers poked into the dough push back elastic.

Forget great-grandpa's need to stop behind a tree, his magic coat pulled aside.

Let dough rise until doubled in bulk. Punch down.

Let rest and rise.

Let rest.

Let rest.

* * *

First Song #5

Little feet be careful
where you lead me to
Anything for Jesus
I would gladly do.

At five years old, I knew Jesus was
- a man in a white bathrobe that would keep me safe in the night
- a man whose daddy (like mine) knew everything I did and didn't like any of it

- a man who died for me so I'd better behave
- a man who loved me, but if I didn't behave, his daddy (like mine) would smite me or send a plague of frogs

How could I ever trust a man? How did I ever learn to trust Charlie?

* * *

"Why don't you want to do Jesus anymore?" my friend asks. "You have all the clothes and papers and books."

"He's been turned into an idol," I answer. "I want another story. One that helps an old woman with a demented husband survive in a Trumpian world."

She looks at the colored pencil drawing that is lying across my lap.

"What's that thing in your picture?"

"What thing?"

"That thing that looks like a white envelope," she says. "The thing inside that green circle."

"I don't know," I reply. Does everything have to be *called* something? Ever since that Hebrew god gave Adam power to name things, we get anxious until we can attach a word to what we're seeing. Then we think we have power over what we've named and limit any further exploration."

"I know you're pissed, but couldn't that envelope have the story you're looking for?"

"Well, maybe. But I'm going to wait and see what emerges."

* * *

"I want you to write my obituary," Mother says.

Oh, no. Here we go with her death plans again.

"I don't want you to tell the truth about me," she continues, pauses, and then adds, "How nasty I was to you kids."

Whaaa!?

Mother sits silent, her arms resting across the table in front of her. She studies her hands, arthritic fingers with joints that point in opposite directions.

Finally recovered enough, I ask, "What do you mean?"

"Oh, I don't know. Just the way I was with you kids."

"What do you remember?" I prompt.

She shakes her head, looks at the plate of chocolate chip cookies I brought, and then says, "Have you talked with Phil lately?"

"No . . . ?"

Is she remembering something she did to my brother? Or changing the subject?

"He is coming over on Saturday."

Okay. We're not pursuing the nasty things she did.

Does she remember how she sacrificed me on her altar of being a good Christian woman?

Does she remember making me take cookies to spooky old lady Borgnis?

Does she remember pulling down my pants, pushing me over the claw foot tub, and spreading my butt cheeks so Marjorie Thostenson can see what worms look like?

Mother is unwilling to unpack any *nasty* memories. I am unwilling to open myself to further emotional abuse. If she's looking for forgiveness, I'm not ready to give it.

Write her obituary? I don't think so.

* * *

The final belief is to believe in a fiction, which you know to be a fiction, there being nothing else. The exquisite truth is to know that it is a fiction and that you believe in it willingly.
— Wallace Stevens

* * *

The only reason I signed up and paid money for this two-day workshop at Green Lake is because I like the presenter's name. Mr. Peter Storey. Word is that Mr. Storey has good ones. I'm looking for a story that will help me navigate being an old woman in a patriarchal culture.

Mr. Storey, a bishop from South Africa, worked with Desmond Tutu and has been invited by my progressive colleagues to address the issue that is threatening to split the United Methodist Church— full ordination rights for our LGBTQ brothers and sisters.

Mr. Storey gets my full attention with his opening statement. "The world is disinterested, disillusioned, and disgusted with Christians. The question isn't whether the church can find a mission," he adds, "but whether God's mission can ever find a church."

I'm in agreement with his brief pronouncement, and within seconds, I'm aware that Mr. Storey is talking about the god who sides with Moses and liberates slaves out of bondage. He claims that same god is on the side of the LGBTQ folks.

But isn't that the god who promised Hebrews a land of milk and honey, led them into an already occupied land, and helped them slaughter the Canaanites, the Hittites, the Perizzites, the Girgashites, the Amorites, the Jebusites?

To name a few.

Isn't that the god who is worshipped by people who are still slaughtering Palestinians in order to have the property they think was promised to them?

Mr. Storey claims that God is on the side of the people who want to be included. Which god is that? I wonder.

* * *

Conversation between Katharine, my church secretary, and her four-year-old son, Joey:

"Mom, what does God look like?"

"I don't know, Joey. What do you think God looks like?"

"I think she looks just like Nancy."

* * *

"You're still involved?" Linda asks, interrupting my complaining about Father God, Jesus, and all the other ubiquitous male idols that parade their power through the worship services.

"Yeah," I answer, swallowing my chagrin at continuing to unload on my friend who gave up on church years ago. "I guess because I want to be with people who recognize there is something bigger than we are."

Where else do people of all ages get together regularly? Where else would I see a tiny baby and know how hard his mom and dad tried to have this child and then talk with the baby's grandmother whose husband died just before the little boy was born?

At least before Covid-19, I could hug my strong women friends, have a cup of insipid church coffee, and laugh about the latest Trump joke.

Thunderdumb, one calls him.

129

* * *

*"If you have to leave a church to save your soul, don't go quietly,
and if you stay, don't stay quietly."*
— Joan Chittister

* * *

What did Rusty and I talk about the morning after Peter died?
Our telephone conversation was brief. She was dealing with the
aftermath of her son's sudden death.

I was dealing with a theological dilemma.

All the old, dead white male European theologians I studied
in seminary rejected God as a puppeteer pulling the strings of our
lives. But what if I hadn't left home that morning at 8:00? What if I
hadn't arrived at Rusty's home an hour earlier than planned? Was
there some crafty cosmic manipulator that decided He (or maybe
She or They) wanted me to be with my dear mentor and friend
when she learned of her son's death?

Why am I driven to discover another story? Another god or
goddess?

"Should I go now?" I'd asked Rusty as the detectives left.

"No. Stay." She said and reached for my hand.

This woman who lent me paper, pastels, and hours of her
presence and power in the psych unit to help me stave off the
demons had now invited me into her sanctuary of grief.

An ineffable gift.

* * *

The mystery of God touches us – or does not – in the smallest details: giving a strawberry, with love; receiving a touch, with love; sharing the snapdragon red of an autumn sunset, with love.
— Marion Woodman

* * *

Who wrote the phrase, *my childhood bends beside me*? Lucky that their body only bends. My childhood jumps out of nowhere, seizes my whole body, and rattles my gray cells into the 1940s. Like now, when I'm on the fence about continuing my involvement at church.

I'm trying to discern whether I should put up with the preponderance of patriarchal pap or become a born-again pagan like Rusty. But as soon as the fence metaphor pops up, I'm a kid, standing in the back yard near the flaking white paint on the picket slats around the 707 Blaine Street garden.

My father is there, hoeing the carrots. Moments earlier, he found the nest of baby rabbits underneath the lettuce and hacked them into bloody fur oblivion.

There are no tomatoes. My father doesn't like them. He says the seeds get stuck in his teeth, and because my father, like Father God, is in charge, I don't taste tomatoes until I am 18 and my new husband urges me to at least try a bite of one.

Now during worship, Father God and his male pronouns show up dozens of times in prayers, hymns, and creeds. Although I substitute a few shes and hers while singing, I still leave the church with a mouth full of annoying seeds.

131

* * *

The congregation belts out a favorite old hymn, one I know by heart. Anticipating the second verse before it begins, I look at Charlie. He catches my eye, and we both grin as we sing, *Here I raise mine Ebenezer, hither by thy help I'm come.*

Our grin is a smug grin because we're sure most of the worshipers are probably thinking of Scrooge and don't know ebhen ha-'ezer means "Stone of Help." But Charlie and I know about Samuel picking up a rock to thank his god for the victory against the Philistines.

Although Samuel's Ebenezer is probably only interesting to another pastor, the reference immediately connects me to this man at my side. A man who, long before I fell in love with him, helped me with seminary papers. And a man who now often can't remember my name, asks the same question three times within two minutes, puts his dirty dishes back in the cupboard, and dumps chicken bones in the recycle bin.

Even before the hymn is over, I'm washed white with shame at my impatience with Charlie's confusion. Too often my impatience gives way to anger. I wail. Moan. Stand sobbing in the shower until hot water hitting my head quells my rage.

While the congregation is settling down for prayer, I'm thinking that if a stone works for Samuel, my ancient, faith relative, maybe a stone would help me. A stone I could carry in my pocket that would help me calm down and respond to my husband's confusion with kindness instead of meltdowns. A special stone. One that holds meaning for Charlie and me.

But what stones do we have?

A slab of trilobites from the five-mile creek of his childhood? Too big.

A hunk of rock from Machu Picchu? Too rough and would tear my pocket.

The Petoskey stone? Ah. Perfect. A smooth, half-dollar-sized stone covered with tiny hexagonal fossils that Charlie and I found in Michigan. We were crazy in love then and fascinated by the designs we discovered in each other as well as the patterns on the stone.

At home after church, determined to deal with my explosive temper and recover my affection for my husband, I look through cabinets, drawers, and boxes for the Petoskey stone. After an hour, disappointed, I give up my search and fix lunch for Charlie and me.

Later in my office, I notice the chipped and dented tin box that years before had held Lebkuchen, a German cookie made with honey. Instead of my hoped-for Petoskey stone, the tin holds a clown nose, a dried-up blue highlighter, two copper book marks from Santiago, and a small, white bag with Amsterdam Sauer, the name of a gem store, written across the front.

I remember that tiny bag. Another happy time with Charlie. A happy *legitimate* time on a river trip from Amsterdam to Vienna. The bag is a gift from a salesman who comes onto the tour boat hoping to lure tourists into his shop.

The polished stone that falls out of the bag is a deep magenta color about the size of an apricot pit. Still tucked into the bag is a small paper. I unfold and read:

Agate. Considered a powerful talisman by many ancient civilizations, this genuine Brazilian gemstone is mainly associated to calm and balance. To give luck and positive energies, this charm must always be given as a gift. So this is our gift to you! We wish you great energies! Amsterdam Sauer.

A gift. A gift of calm and balance. Perfect.

I stick the talisman in my pocket.

* * *

Meditation

"Picture a log floating down a river," Larry-the-guru said. "As thoughts come into your head, put the thought on the log and it will disappear downstream. Another thought will come. Another log will show up. Just keep letting your thoughts float away. The idea is to train your mind to focus."

I try meditating. My thought: What's for breakfast? Eggs? Multigrain toast? Last night's pizza? Oh. Here comes a log. It's about three feet long and has a short branch with a little green leaf on the end. Wow. It's floating on past me like Larry said.

Aw. The little green leaf is waving at me. Oh, shit. It's heading for some raging rapids!

Whoops. Here comes another log. It's dragging a picket fence behind it.

There was a picket fence around the garden at 707 Blaine Street. Mother planted carrots, lettuce. No tomatoes. My father didn't like . . . oh, no.

I'm back on the fence.

Should I stay in the church? Pick-et the Jesus story?

Crap. Now I'm into puns. Scattered thoughts. "Monkey Mind," Larry-the-guru called it.

Get another log.

Wait. What kind of monkey? Maybe Darwin, the spider monkey. The kids found him hiding behind our furnace. Crawling along the . . .

Damn. Damn. Where are these logs coming from? I could build a cabin. Maybe by this river. Over there underneath the weeping willow. Do some fishing . . . Oh, hell . . . I give up.

* * *

"Why do you keep going?" Linda asks during our once a week breakfast date. For almost 30 years, we've shared stories about our jobs, grief about my grandson's death and her nephew's suicide, our husbands' idiosyncrasies, and Packer scores. Today, between bites of Belgian waffle, I'm whining *again* about male language during worship.

"I don't know why," I answer. "Maybe because I don't know how to leave."

Linda swallows more coffee and then says, "I have a client who was raised Catholic. She says she goes to church for the community. She says she doesn't pay any attention to the male language. She's made some good friends," Linda continues. "She enjoys working with them, making sandwiches for the homeless shelter."

On the way home, I think about my strong women friends at North Pointe United Methodist Church. They don't care that God is a Father with a Savior Son. They're not bothered with hymns, creeds, and prayers that perpetuate male domination. They walk in the Black Lives Matter protests, serve on school committees, work at the food pantry, sew pillowcases for the homeless shelter, organize "Relay for Life," and make quilts for pregnant teens.

Those friends listen politely to my opinions about the power of words and then talk about which Thai restaurant has the best Pad See Ew.

What's the matter with me?

* * *

135

What they have in common (people engaged in holy work, not necessarily members of a church) is an acute sensitivity to the brokenness of other people and a willingness to participate in their healing.
— Barbara Brown Taylor, *Christian Century*, June 1999

* * *

March 14

Well, I made it to 80. A weird-looking spiked virus upset my plans to treat my women friends to dinner at Sebastian's in Racine. Instead, some of my family members, plus one friend, courageously met for a lunch at Aria, one of the restaurants at St. Kate The Arts Hotel in Milwaukee.

Now we are all home and following CDC suggestions for avoiding death.

Which story did I tell myself to make it to 80? What story did I tell myself to make it through today?

* * *

*When you die, you don't go away from the world,
the world goes away from you.*
— Doug Flaherty

* * *

The world started going away from me in 1985, but I didn't notice until my first husband bought a computer and put it in the only extra room we had. The room in which I meditated.

I tried to get rid of my anger about his invading my space and buying another toy (to go along with the stereo, the new car, and a second boat). He offered to teach me, but I resisted—out of anger and stubbornness—to learn anything from him. I kept using the easy and reliable Royal Electric to print sermons and newsletters.

As the years unfolded, the computer stealthily insinuated itself into the parsonage, the church office, and my bank. Dragged kicking and screaming into the 21st century, I succumbed to the rapid usurpation of technological wonders when two of my children ambushed me at a fancy garden lunch with a "Get an iPhone, Mom," intervention.

These days my son and grandson happily show me the latest marvels on iPhone. The cleaning woman shows me a funny clip on Instagram comparing Obama and Trump in their announcements of killing ben Laden and Abu Bakr al Baghdadi. I laugh, but I don't want to spend the time to figure out Instagram. Or Pinterest, Facebook, or Twitter. One friend only texts. Another only Messengers. Whatever that is.

My present husband and I keep the landline because we're bundled or something and would have to pay an extra $40 a month *not* to have that something. No one calls on the landline except someone named Nancy, who calls every day—one day *nine* times—to tell me I'm going to lose my Medicare if . . . I don't know the "if" because I hang up.

The smart TV remote is a mystery. Only one finger is needed, but that finger had better press the right buttons. I use my index finger.

I'm saving my middle finger for people who call me a dinosaur.

* * *

Karen called this morning to wish me a happy birthday and gave me an update on our high school friends. "Alice died. Jo is in memory care, and Mary's arthritis keeps her from going out much."

Why did I laugh?

We're all turning 80 this year. I'm wondering how to be an old woman in a Trump World, and my childhood friends are worried about taking their next breath.

* * *

I don't feel old.
I don't feel anything until noon and then it's time for a nap.
— Bob Hope

* * *

A brief paragraph in this morning's *Racine Journal Times* announces a "No Regrets Conference" being held next week at a local church. The $30, one-day event is for men ages 13 and older who are choosing to walk toward a lifetime of faith in Jesus.

No REGRETS? What kind of an impossible promise is that? Sounds like *Love means never having to say you're sorry.*

My first husband believed all that shit.

* * *

Charlie and I began "Safer at Home" isolation today. Two days ago I turned 80, and 50 years ago, I was put into a locked room at St. Elizabeth's.

Another isolation.

This morning I got a pattern for a mask off the Internet and spent the afternoon sewing masks so that we could go vote.

"Are we the only ones here?" Charlie asked while we were eating supper.

"Yes."

"What about that person in the basement?"

"What person in the basement?"

"There was someone down there this afternoon."

"That was me, Charlie. I was sewing masks."

* * *

If I hesitate writing coronavirus, the little autocorrect guy quickly suggests *crowbar.*

Don't we have a crowbar? While I'm waiting to see if the virus finds me, I could look for the crowbar.

Wikipedia says the name "crowbar" was suggested by the shape of the bird's beak and feet. The description also included the tool being called a "jammy" or "jimmy" when a crowbar is used for a burglary.

My brain is scrambled in this uncertain Covid-19 time.

Jammy? I bought a new pair for my sleep apnea study.

Jimmy? My boyfriend in fourth grade who I let ride my new bike down the Blaine Street hill.

I need a crowbar to extricate myself from my so-called life. A childhood life that is filled with burdensome stories. And the present one. Sheltered in the house with a husband who wants to go home.

* * *

Until reading the *New York Times* weekend arts section this morning, I had never heard of St. Rosalia. Turns out that during a 1624 plague in Palermo, a few Franciscans dug up some bones in a hill near the harbor. The archbishop declared they must be the remains of St. Rosalia, dead for centuries. When the saint's relics were carried through the quarantine city, the Palermitani began recovering.

It was a miracle!

Anthony van Dyck, while caught in the quarantined city, painted pictures of the saint. One of the five paintings remaining—*St. Rosalie Interceding for the Plague-Stricken of Palermo*—was one of the first paintings acquired by the Metropolitan Museum of Art and was to be the centerpiece of the museum's 150th birthday celebration planned for March 30.

Three days from now.

But guess what? St. Rosalia (or St. Rosalie—the article does not explain two spellings), is quarantined along with the museum.

And all the rest of us.

"*Viva Palermo e Santa Rosalia!*" a celebratory crowd shouted every year as an image of the city's savior was paraded through Palermo.

While we're waiting for more masks, ventilators, and a flattened curve, couldn't we find some old, dead saint bones we could carry through Racine?

* * *

Day #34 of "Safer at Home." Politicians are looking for someone or something to blame for Covid-19. They fasten on Wuhan, China. Was the virus on wild animal meat in the city's "wet market?" Did the germ escape from a lab a few blocks away? How about the natural phenomenon that folks have been fearing for several years?

No one is considering that Grandmother Goddess Hannahannah might be responsible. Maybe she heard Greta Thunberg address the United Nations on September 23 last year, saw the ho-hum response to her call to action about our climate change peril, and got really pissed.

When Hannahannah gets angry, she heads to the underworld.

On January 1, while humans were dancing and drinking in the New Year, Hannahannah shut down her iMac, picked up her luggage, and slipped through the veil of light and dark.

Of course, during the six months of every year that Hannahannah is underground, everything above goes to hell.

And she doesn't care.

Especially *this time* she doesn't care.

She knows that an abused Mother Earth needs a break.

So in her underground suite, Grandmother Goddess Hannahannah lies back on feather pillows and thinks while she's here that maybe she'll take ukulele lessons.

* * *

I finally found a goddess that will answer me. By email. Imagine. Her name is Mary. Not the Virgin Mary whom everybody sings about this time of year, but my Mary my friend who is in a second marriage, wears a heart monitor, and has issues with her computer.

Someone who understands me.

She responded within hours of my latest turmoil with my demented husband.

My email to Mary: I snap. I've learned to answer the same question up to the fourth time within two minutes, and I can pick the chicken bones out of the recycling bin, but when he answered the phone and told the solicitor from his Alma Mater to put him down for $440, I screamed.

I wailed. Just last week I spent hours with him going over and over the benevolence list that *he* created early in our marriage. We had already paid Ohio Wesleyan $440 this year and both decided to cut the pledge for 2020 to $400. He graduated 60 years ago! When the caller ID showed up in the left-hand corner of our smart TV during *Wheel of Fortune,* I told him *not* to answer the phone.

Mary-the-Goddess emailed me back: I'm so sorry. I have no idea how stressful your life is with Charlie's constant confusion, but I know you are strong and will get the business of gifting money to his college all straightened out. I am certain that by calling them, you can explain the situation and adjust your gift to the "plan."

I respond via email: Thank you!

Not one of those ancient goddesses ever contacted me with support.

* * *

The billboard message along highway 41 advises: *Jesus is the answer. What is your question?*

My questions:

Who killed Jamal Khashoggi?

Who created Covid-19?

Who is going to show up at my door with a box of Turkish Delights?

Maybe the Jesus-Is-The-Answer question helps render him obsolete? Maybe he's tired of feeling responsible for all the guilt that's been piled on people for 1,500 years.

* * *

'The finger points toward the moon;' thus starts a Zen saying. The eyes move from the finger to the moon—and they see. But if the skies are clouded, if there is no moon to be seen, then the finger will not do. The eyes will turn to the cloudy skies, but they will not see anything.

'Moon,' someone says.

And the moon shines inside the soul, even if it is
absent from the skies . . .
— Rubem Alves, The Poet, The Warrior, The Prophet

* * *

What do I do with Jesus now? When during those 50 years did his name lose its power? How do I have the audacity to be looking for another story when Jesus-the-Word pulled me out of the St. Elizabeth womb and resurrected me into a new life?

What moon-words do I need now to save Charlie and me from this crazy coronavirus that has us locked into our home?

* * *

What are we without the help of that which does not exist?
— Paul Valery

* * *

143

For two years, I've been trying to find a different story than Jesus. Something that will help me navigate a patriarchal world in which Trump is in charge. My plan to consult goddesses got out of hand, and now I never know who is going to show up. Jesus who wants me to quit messing up his story? My mother who wants me to do another piece on her strength?

This morning it was Hannahannah. She wanted to know where the hell I'd been for six months. She thought maybe I'd taken a cue from her and slipped underground.

"I'd completely understand," she said. "Trump and all. But you've left me dormant since last May. Why did you quit your morning routine with that electronic storytelling machine?"

Glad that Hannahannah showed up instead of Jesus, I answered, "I was working on Step #6 in Maureen Murdock's heroine journey."

"What is that?"

"Initiation and descent to the goddess."

"Huh?"

"You are the oldest goddess I've discovered and a grandmother to boot, but hundreds of goddesses have showed up since you. They all dragged their stories along with them."

"Good stories?"

"Oh, my, yes!"

"Any stories that satisfy your search?"

"No. I'm beginning to suspect my own story is what I have to deal with."

* * *

Mother hovers over this iMac keyboard, directing my fingers like I am anxiously skidding a planchette over a Ouija Board. She suggests I see her through her good Christian woman lens. "Take this envelope to the Connors," Mother says. "It's for Baby Stewart."

Mother is enlisting me again in a neighborhood ritual. At the time of death, "the envelope" gets passed from house to house and the collected donations are given to the grieving survivors.

A few days earlier, Baby Stewart was the centerpiece on our dining room table. "He's a blue baby," my mother said, preparing me as Stewart's mother knocks on our back door. "He probably won't live very long."

Hugging a bundle of blankets, our next-door neighbor places her package on our dining room table and unwraps her temporary gift. Stewart's swaddling clothes fall in designed folds onto our lace tablecloth. His tiny body is at my five-year-old eye level.

I had imagined a baby the shade of "sky blue" in my Crayola Box of 64, but Stewart's skin is dove gray, the color of Grandma's good dishes. The only blue on Stewart is the edging of his sleeper and tiny jagged veins beneath his skin's surface, like finger shadows when fine porcelain is held up to the light.

Stewart, a firstborn child, makes no crying or sucking noises. Just like my doll, Carol Ann, whose eyelids automatically swing shut when her limp body is prone, Stewart is silent. As my mother and his mother talk quietly in the kitchen, I study Stewart's face for a sign of life. Hope swells when I think I see a shallow movement in one nostril.

Never included in important conversation, I am silent, too, when I overhear my mother tell my father that Stewart died.

At the moment in which Stewart lies center table top death is close. About two feet away, I figure. At five years old it's the closest I've been to death. Someone else's death, that is.

* * *

145

You've Had It

You can't understand why Donald isn't being impeached
or fired or whatever they're doing now with sexual abusers

You can't understand how Roy Moore can run for office
and refer to Mary and Joseph to excuse his pedophilia

You can't understand why Christians can't see the connection
between a god they call Father and men being in charge of everything

Including women.

* * *

Inanna, the Sumerian Queen of Heaven, showed up again. I
spent an hour reading *The Descent of Inanna*, a 415-verse poem with
a huge cast of characters. She wants to go underground to attend the
funeral of her brother-in-law.

Big mistake. When she gets there her jealous sister, Ereshkigal,
Queen of the Underworld, kills her and hangs her up on a hook
"like a rotting piece of meat." But no worries. Inanna's daddy-god
resurrects her with the help of two sexless beings he creates from
the dirt under his fingernails.

Imagine. A death and resurrection of a *female* 3,500 years *before*
Jesus.

But Inanna's story doesn't end there. It gets better.

Ereshkigal is pissed that her sister is alive again and insists she
won't allow Inanna back into the upper world without providing a
substitute.

The substitute Ereshkigal wants is Inanna's husband, Dumuzid.

Here's where the story gets really important. Enter Dumuzid's sister, who sacrifices *herself* to save her brother.

A sacrificial *woman*? Though she's barely mentioned in Inanna's poem, this woman has a name: Geshtinanna.

I *love* her! So what if she's a goddess. She *sacrifices* her life. So what if it's for a man. She *sacrifices*!

Yes. I know. Women have been sacrificing ever since Eve's mother, but until Geshtinanna, I didn't have a heavenly rep.

Geshtinanna. Inanna. Hannahannah. What's with the anna anna annas?

* * *

And we are put on earth a little space,
that we may learn to bear the beams of love.
— William Blake

* * *

Did I learn the "I can't. I can. I will." chant while helping at that religious studies I course? Who got me to agree to provide food and prepare meals for 11 kids and three adults while the kids' parents were participating in the weekend workshop?

And who saw me sitting down in the kitchen when the Sloppy Joe goop was ready way ahead of lunchtime and commandeered me into the next room where the kids were all singing "Life is full of ups and downs, ups and downs, ups and downs . . . "

The tune was "London Bridge." The last line, which I can't remember, was certainly *not* "my fair lady."

Jesus must have been in the last line somewhere.

After they finished the song, the leader taught the chant: "I can't. I can. I will."

Later I learned the simple triplet was the Christian faith simplified.

Father God's creation puts *I can't* limits on my human agency, i.e. cancer, tornados.

Jesus Christ proclaims that *I can* choose among options that are always present in the midst of any circumstance, i.e., medication, hide in the basement.

And if I decide *I will* act on one of the options, the Holy Spirit will sustain me, i.e., chemo, home insurance.

These dementia days when I reach the pinnacle of my patience and am ready to jump off into the chasm of despair, I scream, "I can't. I can't *do* this. I can't" and break down and sob. Echoes of the chant I learned 50 years ago and never forgot shame me into further hopelessness.

Charlie, of course, is remorseful. He thinks he's done something wrong and is effusively sorry. "Can you forgive me?" he says. Over and over. Much too soon.

I *can't* reach the I *can*. I'm nowhere near the *I can*.

Later, after I hug Charlie and try to assure him that he is not to blame, I realize I am more than *willing* to continue loving him.

I *want* to.

∗ ∗ ∗

Mother is here again. My colleague, Judith, said mothers are easier to love dead. Is Mother pleading with me to discover my love for her? Or has she teamed up with Hannahannah and Rusty to help me learn how to navigate old age in a patriarchal culture?

* * *

*"... know something Sugar? Stories only happen to
the people who can tell them."*
— Lucy Marsden in *Oldest Living Confederate Widow Tells All*

* * *

"You cancelled your 1:00 appointment?" I ask Mother. "Couldn't you find someone to give you a ride?" Guilt *rides* in with my question. I live too far away to provide necessary transportation.

My mother is almost 93 and has mega amounts of health issues. The latest one is kidney failure, and her primary physician, Dr. Betts, referred her to a urologist, whose office is in Janesville, 12 miles from Mother's home.

"I can get a ride," Mother answers. "I just decided I didn't want to see him."

"So, you cancelled?"

"Yes, let's just let things take their course."

I'm still considering her word *let's* and its implication that I'm somehow included in her decision, when she adds, "And the nurse agrees with my philosophy. That doctor does dialysis, and I wouldn't do it anyway."

What? This is new.

While I'm mulling over what to say next, Mother sits back in her swivel rocker. The rose-colored velveteen chair that is faded and worn out at the edges. The rocker that sits in the place where a lift chair would have gone if she hadn't told us to "just forget about that lift chair" because she doesn't want to cause her kids trouble.

"Does Dr. Betts know that you cancelled the appointment?"

149

"No."

"He referred you, didn't he?"

"My nurse says I'm okay."

"Is your nurse in touch with him?"

"When she comes."

"Isn't that nurse a physical therapist?"

"No. She takes my blood pressure. Other things."

I don't ask Mother about the other things because she would just say she has "little problems." One of her little problems is a nasty-looking toilet, which the nurse obviously doesn't take care of. A task for me before I go home. After I get the button sewed on her sweater and her funeral plans changed. Again.

"Do you have the information you need about kidney failure?" I ask.

"The nurse tells me."

"Did she tell you what your options are? What will happen if your kidney function doesn't get better?"

"Well, I'm almost 93. We know what it will mean."

"You mean death," I say, surprised that I have no discomfort at stating the obvious.

Mother does not respond. She sets her lips together and looks straight ahead and out the window at the soggy, gray sky.

Why do I keep interrogating her? She has obviously taken care of her body for 93 years. She has survived death of a spouse and great-grandsons, fires, macular degeneration, crippling arthritis, a knee replacement, a perforated ulcer, two pacemakers . . .

. . . and me.

She lingers on.

"Okay," I say, breaking the silence. "It's your body. You get to make the decisions."

I think my pronouncement settles some kind of sparring that's going on, but even as I relax back into the lumpy couch cushions, scenes of pastoral visits to dying church members begin to flash, and I continue my badgering.

"Do you know what kind of a death?"

"It can't be too bad."

"Yeah, it could be."

I'm petulant now. The warring is within me. What do I want from my mother?

"I don't want my kids to worry about me," my mother says. "I worry about my kids worrying," she adds, deftly throwing the focus away from her and onto me.

"I'm not worried," I say, with an edgy bite. "I know you are getting good care, but I want to know what is likely to happen."

"I'm just going to let things take their course," she repeats.

"But I'd like information," I say, almost whining.

And there it is. I'm in the dining room of 707 Blaine Street, overhearing my mother on the telephone with my grandmother. They are talking about my grandpa who is in the Edgerton hospital. I hear the word cancer, and my stomach shocks into a twisted knot. I will never be told directly about Grandpa's illness. The last time I see him, he has thrown the sheet off his body and I see his legs, skin stretched near splitting, like rotting yellow squash in Grandma's garden. Already at nine years old, I'm too frightened to ask my mother about something upsetting.

"I'll ask Dr. Betts the next time I see him." Mother's answer to my need for information interrupts my memory and is clearly meant both to satisfy me and close the subject of her health.

She doesn't know that I'm dealing with my health now. My insatiable and often denied need for information. When did I learn how to ask questions for answers that I needed simply to get through the day? And when did I get the courage to ask for information that I was afraid might cause anger or tears?

Mother, of course, always wins whatever word skirmish we're in. But her unmovable preservation of self helps me find my own self-information.

* * *

Hell and heaven and good and evil were invented by the left-brain patriarchal culture. In the era of Goddess worshipping the underworld was not a place of punishment, but a place of purification, healing, and preparation for rebirth. The dark was not evil but a part of our cyclical nature.
— Author unknown

* * *

I wonder who found Hannahannah. Which archeologist gently brushed soft bristles across her breasts to uncover her? How long did it take for researchers to figure out she was a grandmother goddess? A crone. Who discovered that she went underground for six months of the year and while she was lolling on feather pillows in the dark, plants above her didn't grow, mother's milk ran dry, and pitiful children cried for food.

Hannahannah. Inanna. Persephone. So many goddesses spend time underground. Usually their "time out" has something to do with seasons and fertility.

What would happen now if I took a break? If I walked out the door, got in the HondaHonda, and headed west?

* * *

First Song #6

Little Feet be careful
Where you lead me to
Anything for Jesus
I would gladly do.

OMG. An awful thought. What if I'm writing this "womb" thing for *Jesus*? What if *he* is the one continually poking pins in the cushions of my brain?

I hope he's not punishing me for questioning his Holy Hypostasis. Maybe he wants my help. Maybe he is looking for a goddess, too. Or another god. Someone to share love with.

Or maybe he's sick of being turned into an idol—worn as jewelry, stuck in plaster statues and stained-glass windows, or, heaven forbid, made out of 635 tons of reinforced concrete on the top of Mount Corcovado, where he gets struck by lightning and can't rest his arms.

If Jesus is prodding my search, will I continue looking?

* * *

What we are looking for is what is looking.
— St. Francis of Assisi

* * *

Although my snarky excuse for entering seminary was to get out of Appleton, what I really wanted was explore the Jesus stories for myself. My quest got complicated during Christology class. All of a sudden, way too many theories by way too many old white northern European men. All of which I had to explicate on exams, all of whose theologies I had to demonstrate proficiency in, and, all of which required that I believe Jesus died for me.

Oh, and he died for everyone else, too. Like the two women who preceded me into the Dynasty Restaurant several weeks ago. Did they hold the door open for me? Of course not. I tell myself that Jesus died for them, too. Doesn't help.

Thirty-five years later, I still don't know what I believe about Jesus.

Again, I share my dilemma about Jesus with my pastor friend, Don. Because of Covid-19, our conversation is through Gmail rather than the church office. I comment on his Zoomed Sunday sermon during which he proclaimed the divine presence within every cell of the universe. I challenge his use of the *name* Jesus.

"I can't do *Jesus*," I write. "I'm aware of some spiritual reality in me, but I can't name it Jesus. The image changes."

"The Wise Old Woman is the Christ in you," Don responds, referring to the muse that has shown up to help me when I was stuck writing sermons.

"Oh," I type. "You used a different *word*. You changed the word *Jesus* to the word *Christ*. The *word* Christ to me is a word that puts a name on that part of me within me that isn't me, but the word still evokes an image of *male*."

I sound like I'm speaking in tongues.

"Christ is Greek for anointed," Don replies, reverting to his professor role. "You definitely are anointed."

Anointed?

What does that mean?

Obviously the issue for me is *words*. I am caught trying to define the ineffable within and around me.

The word *mystery* works for me at this moment.

Mystery.

My-stery.

My Story.

Which one?

* * *

What people are ashamed of usually makes a good story.
— F. Scott Fitzgerald

* * *

I'm doing the Tuesday *New York Times* crossword puzzle at the kitchen table. Charlie is standing nearby and asks, "Do you do those things every day?"

"Only the easy days," I grin.

"My wife does those every day," he says and then asks, "Are we going anywhere?"

"No." *Who does he think I am?*

"I saw your black thing there and wondered if we were going out." *My black thing is the iPhone.*

"No. We're not going out. We're staying in. No one is going out."

"What? No one?"

"Only people going to a grocery store or a drug store?"

"Really?"

"Yes. I've told you." *I can feel myself beginning to lose it.* "There is a virus that is dangerous. Especially for old people."

"What? I haven't heard of such a thing."

"I've told you." *I'm losing it . . .* "Dozens of times. You read the newspapers every day. The newspapers are full of it. You don't listen to me." *I'm not supposed to say "you." I'm supposed to own my feelings or distract him.*

I grab the three newspapers that are still on the table and read the headlines. Loudly.

Wisconsin strips to essentials

Wisconsin nurses: "We are unprepared."

Churches, families, factories rally to create medical masks

'Safer at Home' order coming

Eviction hearings delayed

To some, cost of prolonged isolation is too high

Charlie listens.

"Do you understand?"

"Yes."

"What do you understand?" *I'm being cruel now. I should be arrested for elder abuse.*

"There's a situation."

"What situation?" *I can't quit. I want to quit. I can't. I can't.*

Charlie stands quietly at the table, eyebrows squinched into a question. Waiting.

"There's a *virus!*" *I'm shouting.* "I'll write it down." I wrest the magnetic dry erase board from the refrigerator and write in big blue letters: *CORONAVIRUS.*

"Now do you get it?" *Tears of anger are filling my eyes.*

Charlie's answer is calm. Soft. "Not really. I don't know what that word is."

He is leaning against the wall in the hallway, waiting for me to quit sobbing and get out of the shower.

* * *

Hannahannah. You're back *again*? Why? Every time I look to you for help, you remind me of your six-month underground *retreat.*

"Take a break," you advise.

Easy for you to say. You don't seem to care about your children or grandchildren. You don't have a husband who doesn't remember where the bedroom is. You don't have to make sure the estimated tax check is written and sent.

While you are underground, things above go to hell.

Like now.

Is this pandemic your fault?

I'd love a break. I'd love a cup of coffee at Mocha Lisa with a friend. Hell, I'd love a morning without having to explain Covid-19 over and over and over to my husband.

* * *

Covid Day #51. I'll meet with Truda at noon in the entryway of Shorelight Memory Care and ask questions, sign papers, write a check, and make a list. I'll wear a mask.

I have three days to pack Charlie's clothes, toiletries, and some reading materials and talk with him about going to Shorelight. I'll remind him of our conversation on Sunday as we begin watching the virtual worship service on our iMac.

"Where is that?" Charlie asks.

"At North Pointe."

"I'm going down there."

"There isn't anyone there now. This service was recorded yesterday."

"I'm going." Charlie stands up from the couch.

"You can't." I say. *Shit. I'm not supposed to say 'you can't' I'm supposed to redirect.*

"I'm a pastor!" Charlie shouts angrily. "I want to be with my people!"

I finally get it. Charlie's uncharacteristic volume stuns me into understanding that Charlie sees himself as a pastor first. A husband and father second. His vehement claim provides me with the rationale I need to convince him that Shorelight is a perfect place for him. His positive personality and empathetic listening skills may attract people to him. Maybe he will have a place to fulfill his pastoral role.

* * *

Inventory at age 80

My uterus?

Gone.

but I can remember the names and birthdays of the four people who squeezed out of it on their way to life.

My gall bladder, left cornea, and original knee joints?
Succumbed to age.
but I still have two feet, 10 fingers, and a digestive system
(though it twists and leaks and throws its wait [yes, WAIT!]
around.)
My brain?
Clogged with dusty detritus of useless dates, numbers, and
song lyrics:

- January 3   Birthday of my first boyfriend and the day
his brother found their dad hanging
in the chicken coop
- 409-R   Phone number during childhood, a party line
with Christophersons, Muffleys, and Braehms
- Song Lyrics   "I Saw Esau Sittin' on a Seesaw" by the Ames
Brothers

My heart?
Broken on May 7, 2020: the day I left my husband, Charlie, at
Shorelight Memory Care.

* * *

As above
so below
As within
so without
As the universe
so the soul.
— Hermes

* * *

My older daughter arranged a 45-minute session for me with Selah-the-psychic. Selah asked me to send two questions and gave me a choice of two dates when she would send her reading through email.

My choice: July 1, 2020.

My questions:

1. What would help me survive as an 80-year-old woman in a Covid-19 patriarchal world?

2. My husband recently was admitted to a memory care facility. How do I manage living alone after 30 years of marriage?

On my chosen day, Selah's soothing voice ripples through Hulu.

"Your mind is a temple for sacred things that serve you and the world in community," she purrs. "You are delighted and surprised with spiritual things. Your curiosity helps you survive."

She advises asking for help with what I need without feeling unworthy.

Right.

She claims there is deep wisdom from another life breaking in, trying to get my attention. She doesn't describe exactly *how* that wisdom is attempting to get through my addled days. And my feelings of unworthiness prevent me from asking.

I've been ready for over two years for some help navigating being an old woman in a Trumpian world, and I'm supposed to survive with only curiosity?

* * *

Another goddess found me this afternoon. She has red hair, wears a romping giraffe on her auburn swede vest. She lives near the water, swims through the deaths of her children, paints grief in pastel words on Bahamian paper, and comes to me in waves.

160

She had to die before I felt her love for me.
Birth hurts.

* * *

You and I can never be born enough. We are human beings for whom birth is a supremely welcome mystery. The mystery of growing happens only whenever we are faithful to ourselves.
— e e cummings

* * *

My brother, Phil, and I leave Mother's hospital room after another visit. She has survived a perforated ulcer, knee replacements, two pacemakers, macular degeneration, crippling arthritis, and now her 93-year-old heart and kidneys are failing.

"She's never going to die," I say.

"She says she's ready."

"Oh? I haven't had that kind of conversation with her."

"She thinks she's going to see Dad."

"Oh. Okay . . . "

"But he died when she was 55. He won't recognize her." !

* * *

"I'm still with it," Mother brags, after a rapid recital of her birth date, telephone number, and Social Security number to a nurse who enters the room. After several recent ER trips and this latest hospitalization, Mother finally realizes her increasing falls and weakened condition indicates she needs to live in a facility that provides more care than she receives from her friends in the apartment complex, her home for over 22 years.

My siblings and I research options that are available in Edgerton and share our information with her.

"I want to go to the assisted living place," Mother says.

"You have to be able to walk," my sister, Margaret, reminds her.

There is no response from the bed. For two days, Mother has refused to try to walk.

"I talked with the director at Long-Term Care," my brother, Phil says. "There is room there."

"No! I don't want to go there."

Mother is clear this time about what she wants. I don't ask about her intense refusal. She once told me she got a prize for the number of years she served as a volunteer in that hospital unit, and during that time, our lunch conversations often included her complaints about the uncaring decisions made by the management. She must have seen patient neglect or abuse and wanted none of it.

A few days after this conversation, Mother opts for another decision. Her "with it" springs a leak and she dies.

＊ ＊ ＊

Learn first how to live.
Learn second how not to kill.
Learn third how to live with death.
Learn fourth how to die.
— Master Po

＊ ＊ ＊

When did I remember to look in my *Woman's Encyclopedia of Myths and Secrets?* OMG!

Hannahannah sometimes shows up as a virgin who annually imprisons the sacred king in a temple tower, mates with him, then kills him.

Talk about a praying mantis honeymoon.

* * *

Mother, settled in the back seat of my Honda, is silent all the way to Racine. Because I live 75 miles from her, one of my siblings usually provides the transportation Mother needs. But today my brother is busy at work and my sister is afraid Mother's urn will leak, so I volunteer to take the day off and pick her up at the Albrecht Funeral Home and Crematorium.

We arrive at my home in the late afternoon. Snow that has been predicted is beginning to fall. I put Mother on an empty shelf in the garage. She'll be fine there until August, when I'll take her to our family gathering at the Milton Cemetery.

I hear knocking at the back door after supper. I'm in the office, the room furthest from the back door into the garage. A bit nervous at being alone, I hope it's my husband, Charlie, coming home early from his evening meeting. But when he doesn't announce that he's home, I reluctantly decide to check on the noise. Alert for imminent danger, I creep down the hallway, through the kitchen, and into the family room, and slowly open the back door.

Nothing. No serial killer. No clever raccoon. Nothing.

Relieved, I'm settled back in the office when there is knocking again. A strong wind is blowing the snow sideways. Maybe a tree limb is hitting the window in the family room.

When there is nothing, no one at the door, I think, *Maybe it's Mother.* Skeptical of ghosts, I scoff at my own thought and dismiss the possibility.

But there is another knocking.

I give up. Just in case, I take Mother off the cold garage shelf, bring her into the warm family room, and set the thick cardboard box on the soft carpet underneath the desk.

Mother stays there completely silent through the rest of winter, spring, and into summer. In late August, I settle her in my Honda for her last ride to a permanent resting place.

* * *

"We can't keep him anymore," the nurse from Azura says. "He kicks. Tears the window screens. Throws coffee. It took three staff to pull him off a woman he thought was his wife. She was terrified."

No. No. Not another move. I hold back tears.

The nurse continues, "We tried four different places in Milwaukee. No one will take him."

"What do you recommend?" I choke out my question.

"You should try and find a geriatric psych unit. They can help settle him down."

"A what?" A psych unit for old people?

"A geri-psych unit. They'll work to find the right meds."

"Where do I find one?"

"I'll give you a name and number of one I know in Illinois. We sent a woman there, and six weeks later she came back and was fine."

I quit crying long enough to call my friend and tell her I have to bring Charlie home.

She agrees to ride along when I pick him up.

Three staff people, carrying a suitcase, small box, and a mylar balloon, escort Charlie to the car. One helps him into the passenger seat. One hands the balloon to my friend, who is sitting behind Charlie. The third one puts the suitcase and box in the trunk.

"Happy Birthday, Sweetie," I say. Charlie smiles when I tell him it's his birthday. He is quiet for the 20-minute ride home.

He doesn't know who I am.

* * *

The eyes grow dim
The shoulders droop.
Getting old is pigeon poop.
— Source unknown

* * *

3:30 a.m.

Loretta is sitting across from me at the kitchen table. She is here to help take care of Charlie. We have just managed to help him pee in the toilet instead of the closet. He is back in bed asleep.

Loretta and I are awake.

"I've never been in a house where there are two pastors," Loretta says and chuckles.

"Oh?"

"You know," she says, looking askance at me, "the Methodists don't teach the Bible correctly."

"Oh?" Shit. Now what? I don't want to argue with Loretta. She sweeps the floor and does the dishes.

Loretta reaches for her phone. "I have a video for you to watch. It's only eight minutes."

What? Why can't I say no? Go back to bed?

"Just watch this video. You'll see that everything is going to be all right." She swipes her finger across the screen of her phone, pokes a button, and hands it to me.

Just Around the Corner is the title of the video. I find nothing terribly objectionable, but I can feel the threat of a bad religious conversation creeping up my spine.

"You know," Loretta says, "that this struggle you are having will soon be over. The promise is of a beautiful world . . . just like the video says. Right around the corner."

Right around the corner in the bedroom is Charlie, only at home with me until he can be admitted to the geri-psych unit in Bolingbrook.

"Let me show you another video," Loretta says, reaching for her phone. "This one's short."

This video is animated and not short enough for me.

Loretta must see my narrow-eyed, thinly disguised resistance.

"You know," she says, pausing slightly, "it's like you are a woman and your name is Nancy."

Huh?

"And your husband is a man and his name is Charles."

Where in the hell is this going?

She reaches for my hands and speaks firmly.

"And there is *God* and his name is *Jehovah*."

I can't respond.

* * *

The name that can be named is not the eternal name.
— Lao Tzu, *Tao Te Ching*, Chapter 1

* * *

Words trip me up. Like the word *gallimaufry*, a noun used in a review of Joyce Carol Oates new book. 1. A hash made from leftovers. 2. A jumble; hodgepodge.

Before I looked up "gallimaufry" in my 1,550 page *American Heritage Dictionary of the English Language,* I thought it might refer to chickens or a Spanish warship.

I get bogged down with words.

* * *

Hannahannah is getting on my nerves. She showed up again this morning.

"Are you still working on Maureen Murdock's heroine journey Step #6?" she asked.

"Kind of."

"What do you mean 'kind of?'"

"Well, I'm getting tired of goddesses. There are way too many of them, and they end up being taken over completely by male gods."

"Oh. Really? When did *that* happen?"

"It took a while. Mostly when your descendants quit wandering around the Ancient Near East looking for food and figured out how to plant stuff."

"I'm sorry to hear it. I was going to suggest another goddess."

"Please don't! I need to figure out how to make sense out of 160 pages of double-spaced Times New Roman ramblings."

* * *

They whom we love and lose are no longer where they were before.
They are now wherever we are.
— St. John Chrysostom

* * *

The phone rings while I'm driving east on Highway 50 toward Lake Geneva. I recognize the number and answer.

"Charlie passed about 10 minutes ago," Colleen, the hospice nurse, says.

Was I the one who gasped a sharp intake of breath and choked a cry?

"Are you driving?"

"Yes."

"Can you pull over?"

I'm approaching County W. See a driveway. Check the rear-view mirror. An 18-wheeler bearing down in the left lane. I signal. Pull over. Colleen waits while I sob and moan. "It's not fair. This is the *first time* they said I could visit."

"I know. I had just been with Charlie and was on my way home when they called."

"Will I be able to see him?"

"Of course. I'll meet you there."

Colleen meets me at the front door of Burr Oak, the building in which Charlie has died. We're in masks. We don't hug. Charlie is lying on a mat on the floor covered up to his neck in a white sheet. He looks like all dead bodies I have seen. His head tilted back, his mouth agape.

"He wanted to be on the floor," Colleen says, pulling over a chair for me. "We lined this whole room with mats. He slept a lot. When he wasn't sleeping, he folded towels and cloths over and over."

After Colleen leaves, I lean over and brush my hand across Charlie's forehead. Run my fingers through his hair. Gray now. Light brown with highlights of gold in the sunlight when he wrote the poem, set the words to an old hymn tune, and sang to me, "I love to feel your fingers, their touch so soothing up there . . . to know that they are attached to your hands, your arms, do I dare . . . ?

"I'm *so* sorry," I whisper. "I love you. I love you . . .

When the Burr Oak nurse knocks at the door and tells me my 15 minutes are up, I remove his wedding ring from my index finger, the ring given to me by an intake worker at the geriatric psych hospital. "We'll always be together," I promise and put the symbol of our love back in the place he wore it for over 30 years.

Another hospice person meets me at the door, introduces herself, gives me Kleenex, and sits with me at an outside table while I call Charlie's son.

* * *

The greatest human problem is our deep sadness and our greatest human need is to be consoled.
— Abbe Henri Huvelin

* * *

Why do people keep saying *passed* when someone dies? Like they passed a bar exam, or passed gas, or passed a busker in a subway station without throwing a coin into his empty guitar case.

And *pass* where? What world is after this one? At how many funerals did I stand in my Holy Ghost outfit and proclaim the Christian Word of Grace: Jesus said, 'I am the resurrection and the life. Those who believe in me . . . shall never die.'

When asked if I believe in an afterlife, I say. "I don't know. What do you think?"

Charlie didn't pass. Charlie died. Charlie is dead. My truest love is dead.

* * *

love is the every only god
— e e cummings

* * *

Ma'at found me this morning while I was crying for Charlie. Startled by her appearance—her winged arms, her eyes swirled in kohl, and a fluffy feather sticking up from a red head band—my sobs choked dead. She told me she was the daughter of Ra, the sun god, and that she guards creation from chaos and bestows harmony, balance, and interdependence between humans and nature.

Why was she *here*? Was I that out of whack? Screwing up the universe with my grief?

She pointed to the feather on her head and told me that when ancient Egyptians die, their heart is weighed against an ostrich feather. If the heart weighs more than the feather, they will be consumed by the monster Ammit.

Why was she spouting these gruesome details? This couldn't be connected in any way with Charlie. Could it?

170

Finding my voice, I argue.

"I thought a big heart was a good thing," I say. "My husband just died. One of his colleagues sent a sympathy card that included a note—Charlie had a big smile that matched his big heart."

Ma'at doesn't answer. She shrugs and examines her painted fingernails.

"And what about Anne Sexton's "Big Heart" poem?" I whine. "She wrote, 'Big heart, wide as a watermelon.' No scale would be required."

"I can't help you," Ma'at says. "My job is simply to give you information. It's up to you to figure out what to do with it."

She raises her wing-hand above her head, flicks the ostrich feather, and disappears.

I learn it's futile to argue with a goddess. Again.

But what if she's right?

How much does an ostrich feather weigh, anyway?

Using Google and my junior high math, I figure an ostrich feather weighs .04 of an ounce. What about a heart? A heart weighs between eight and 10 ounces, which would mean a whole flock of ostriches plucked nude just to balance the scales.

I'm worried about Charlie. Has some monster already slurped him up?

Or maybe it means that, out of love, Charlie kept giving away pieces of his "big heart" one by one until there was almost nothing left to weigh?

* * *

My writing group meets tomorrow. I've got nothing. I have three open documents on my desktop: Top of the File Cabinet Icons; Did Jesus Have a Belly Button?; and Computer Crap.

Images, ideas, information with lots of "I" words float around in my brain like flotsam and jetsam from Iota the Hurricane. Or was it Ida? Nothing gels.

I'm vomiting these words in an office with a fantastic view of Lake Michigan, and I'm pissed because my coffee is cold, my wrist hurts, and Trump won't concede.

* * *

There can be no liberty for a community that
lacks the means by which to detect lies.
— Walter Lippman

First Song #7

Little feet be careful
where you lead me to
Anything for Jesus,
I would gladly do.

When I was a little kid, Jesus was a character in a book, like Donald Duck and his three nephews: Huey, Dewey, and Louie. My Grandma Bauer, the grandma who fed me brown sugar sandwiches, sat next to me on her maroon mohair couch and read that book over and over and over until I memorized the words, and soon I could read Donald Duck and other books by myself.

That grandmother took me to her Sunday School once. I learned another song:

When he cometh, when he cometh to make up his jewels.
All his jewels precious jewels his loved and his own.
Like the stars of the morning their bright crown adorning,
they shall shine in their beauty bright gems for his crown.

I didn't know who the guy was that was coming, but I sang the
second verse and third verses along with the other children in the
musty church basement:

. . . He will gather, he will gather the gems for his kingdom . . .
. . . Little children, little children who love their redeemer are the
jewels precious jewels his loved and his own.

Me? I'm a little child. Someone loves me? Someone *wants*
me? The taste of those words were sweeter than the brown sugar
sandwiches Grandma fed me.

Later I learned the *he* who loved me was Jesus. The same Jesus
my mother said I had to do anything she wanted me to. Gladly. It
was a trick.

Where is that little girl now? Where is that three-year-old child
who tasted those comforting words that became hidden so deeply
she almost forgot them?

* * *

The quote today in my grandmother's *Longfellow Birthday Book* is:

Oh! This lassitude—this weariness! I have this
morning a singular longing for flowers.
— Hyperion

I had to look up lassitude in my Word Thesaurus.

Yup.

The flowers cost $40, and my jadedness about Trump's desperate and destructive flailing is assuaged.

* * *

While I was fixing breakfast, the photo we took at Nancy's Home Cooking—King Family Owners leapt from its place on the kitchen wall and into the rest of my morning.

Charlie and I found the restaurant early on the day of my writer friend Trudy's funeral. Several nearby options for breakfast were included in the Guide to Columbus in our hotel room, but, of course, we chose the breakfast place because of the name. Charlie and I were pleased with the excellent food, and we left an extra $10 to help offset the cost of meals given to homeless folks who wandered in and were at the church a few minutes before the service began.

Because Trudy and her husband, Elliott, had moved a couple years earlier to the Ohio city, they were not yet well known in the congregation. About 50 people were scattered in clusters of two or three throughout the large sanctuary. Charlie and I slid into an empty pew behind a woman with whom we shared our pack of Kleenex throughout the early part of the service.

The liturgy was the familiar United Methodist Service of Death and Resurrection. Trudy's life was celebrated through prayers, scripture, and reflections from Elliott and a few friends. Earlier I had noticed in the bulletin that communion would be offered toward the end of the service, but I didn't see any evidence of the elements. I was curious to see how this pastor would administer the sacrament.

United Methodists celebrate only two sacraments, baptism and communion, both rituals include promises to receive God's unconditional love that has already been given. Further, during communion, we believe that we are sharing with those who have gone before and those still to come.

Since prohibition and the entrepreneurship of a Methodist named Mr. Welch, no wine is available our denomination's churches. How many times had I worn my Holy Ghost outfit and distributed the bread and grape juice? After so many years, the rubrics and participation in communion had become perfunctory for me.

So when communion was next in the order of the service, I was startled into attention with the pastor's first words. She didn't begin with *The Lord be with you.* She said, "To share this meal, the table must be set." She turned to a small cabinet behind her and, in complete silence, began setting the table as if she was preparing to serve company. Captivated, I watched as she unfolded a white cloth, carefully spread it across the altar, and gently smoothed it with her hands. She continued in silence, placing each symbolic item one by one, carefully and reverently. A silver chalice, a crystal pitcher of juice, a silver paten (the plate holding the bread), and loaf of bread.

While I don't remember how we took communion that day— intinction (dipping the bread in juice) or kneeling at a rail—I began to remember the numerous times Trudy and Elliott had set their table for Charlie and me. The colorful napkins they'd brought from their years in Malaysia. The food served on dishes that Trudy's mother had bought during the last year of World War II, shortly upon arriving in America with six-year-old Trudy after a harrowing escape from Yugoslavia.

During our drive back to Racine, Charlie and I talked about table settings. He still used the plastic Mickey Mouse napkin holder he'd been given as a child. The inserted linen napkin belonged to his mother. He drank milk at every meal from a blue glass he'd bought in Mexico. I described the ugly pastel Melmac set used while the children were little and the Noritake set for 12 that my *then* husband brought back from Japan in 1956. We talked about all the Fiestaware colors. My enjoyment of choosing orange and black on Halloween. Red on Valentine's day. Chartreuse and pink for Easter.

Happy with Biden's win, I used red, white, and blue on January 20, 2021.

How many years have I been setting tables? How many hundreds of family, friends, and neighbors have joined me in a meal?

Now I set the table for myself. This morning, when the kitchen light bounced off the picture of Nancy's Home Cooking—King Family Owners, I remembered Trudy's funeral. I set the table with an antique juice glass given to me by Helen, opened the hutch for a coffee cup saved from Grandma Field's everyday dishes, and lifted my parents' silverplate from the drawer.

With my breakfast ready, I sat a few feet away from the shimmering photo. Remembering again that I was communing with those who had gone before, I looked across the table where Charlie used to sit.

I was not alone.

* * *

2020 Christmas letter

December 1

24 Shopping days until Christmas
261 days since I began Covid-19 isolation
82 days since Charlie died

I count
I count to keep my mind pinned together
during this crazy time

I learned to count from Charlie
who knew how many finches at the feeder
steps to the mail box and miles to the doctor

Though this year he forgot what he'd read
where he lived and who I was
he kept counting until he died

These days I count on people who check on me
help me with techy stuff listen to my whining
and love me anyway

And mostly in these hard times I count on
family and friends to remind me
that love never dies

May love fill your holy-days.

* * *

Rusty showed up early this morning. She just slid open the glass door and stepped into the shower.

Whaa!? I almost dropped the soap. "What are you *doing* here?"

"I want to talk with you about that *careful little feet* thing you are writing. How long have you been sitting at the keyboard sifting through old stories?"

"Almost two years," I stammer, stunned that Rusty knows about my manuscript. Feeling attacked, I add, "My project is not a *thing*. My writing group likes it . . . and *you're* in it.

My wet, defensive deflection doesn't work. "Remind me again," Rusty says. "What prompted you to begin digging up the past?"

"I remember exactly."

Charlie and I are on our way to church. It's late September. He can still drive. He asks, 'Where do you want to sit?'

"Toward the back," I answer. "Near the toilet. My high blood pressure pill kicks in about 9:30."

"Do you care which side?"

I consider. On sunny days, the stained-glass windows that circle around the ceiling of the sanctuary let in the morning sun. As the capricious beams dance across the pews in a rising arc, people on the right side don sunglasses to keep the rays from singeing their eyeballs. But today is gray.

"No," I answer. "I don't care which side. It's clouded over. We won't be blinded by the sun."

"And, there it was," I say to Rusty, who doesn't have a drop of water on her. "I'd spent a lifetime 'blinded by the *son*.' Groping for enlightenment as a woman while bound in patriarchal ligatures.

"At that moment in the car, I wondered how in the hell I was going to survive as an old woman with a husband in early stage dementia."

"So what did you do?"

"I began searching for another story. An archetypal *woman* story. No Jesus."

"Oh, my," Rusty grins. "And how did *that* go?"

"Well, I began exploring goddesses."

"And?"

"It's a bottomless pit. While I was searching for goddesses, all sorts of women showed up. Now you. You're completely dry, but my skin is puckering. I need to get out of this shower."

While I turn off the water and begin to sweep the drops off the dripping doors with that plastic gizmo, Rusty hands me my towel.

"And these two years you've been writing," she continues. "How have *they* gone?"

"Terrible. You died. Charlie died. I turned 80 the same day the Covid-19 lockdown began."

Rusty pauses and then says, "You're still here."

"Yes? What's your point?"

"Well, you survived. How did you do it?"

Rusty's question catches me off guard. I start to answer that I don't know, but before I can get the words out, I remember dozens of people who helped me.

"I had a lot of help," I answer. "I couldn't have survived without support from my children. Charlie's children. Emails and phone calls from Brenda, Mary Ann, Linda. There were women from Home Instead, women from Racine Aging and Disability Resource Center, women from church. Some men, too."

Dry now, I reach around Rusty to hang up the damp towel.

"And, you," I say, "You were a mentor to me, then a friend, and now . . . ?"

"A muse," Rusty says, and quickly adds, "Well, a-mus*ing*."

I laugh, then add to my list of survival techniques, "I also wrote. Almost every day. Just to keep sane."

I lean my head back to put Restasis in my eyes, see Rusty in the mirror, and realize people who are no longer alive—like my mother, grandmothers, goddesses, poets, writers, and Rusty—also helped me survive.

I turn to my dear friend and ask, "Are you here to help me?"

Rusty nods, raises her eyebrows as if she's been waiting all this time for my question, and says, "You've spent over two years looking for ways to survive being an old woman. It's time for you to wrap up your search."

"But . . ."

"I know. You don't think you found any answers, but you've survived. And you have just told me how you've done it."

"What? You mean . . . ?"

"Yes. Go back and reread what you've written. Just look. Maybe in between all the *words* you've set in print, you'll discover the answers you've been looking for."

I bend over to rub lotion on my legs. Old 80-year-old legs, blotched with purple vein lace. When I straighten up, Rusty is gone.

Gone? I wasn't done asking her questions.

Now what?

I trust and love my mentor and friend. Although not certain of her advice, I finish the rest of the eyedrops, do the pills, teeth, and deodorant, and head for my iMac.

I wonder what I'll discover.

* * *

Acknowledgments

And we are put on earth a little space,
that we may learn to bear the beams of love.
— William Blake

William Blake's quote evokes memories of hundreds of people who, for 81+ years, have supported me and helped me learn how to love. To name them would fill a book in itself. I hold them in special places in my heart.

I am especially grateful that my space on earth has included my children and grandchildren, those with whom I share DNA and their partners, and those with whom I share a deep love of their dad and grandfather. Whether they like my stories or not, they have listened, read them, and expressed enough appreciation that I keep on writing.

How can I adequately thank the Friday Round Table group at Red Oak Studio? With Robert Vaughan's leadership, these folks read and critiqued almost every word of *Little Feet*. They laughed and cried along with me. An incredible gift.

I appreciate the careful editing of Kim Suhr, Director of Red Oak Studio, and Carolyn Kott Washburne, Adjunct Associate Professor Emerita, Department of English at the University of Wisconsin-Milwaukee.

Shannon Ishizaki and my publishing team at Ten16 Press have been a delight to work with. Shannon, Sean, Kaeley, and Jayden, my cover illustrator, have listened carefully and exceeded my *Little Feet* (and the rest of me) expectations. Thank you.

Finally, I want to thank my husband, Charles, who died during the writing of *Little Feet*. More than anyone, for over thirty years Charlie helped me learn to bear the beams of love. His love lives on.

Nancy Bauer-King is an eighty-year-old retired United Methodist clergywoman who is exploring her troubled relationship with religious imagery and ideology with humor and, hopefully, honesty.

The title *Little Feet Be Careful* comes from a short song she sang in Sunday School at five years old and appears seven times in the book, each time with a different reflection. Though some of her "stepping" through these past two years of questioning has not been "careful," with help from family and friends, she has survived the pandemic and her husband's death from dementia.

Nancy's fiction and poetry can be found in several anthologies and magazines, such as *Creative Wisconsin Anthology 2018*, *The Christian Century 2019*, and *Wisconsin Poet's Calendar 2020*. She is also the author of *Madness to Ministry* (a memoir) and *The Word From the Wise Old Woman* (a feminine book of sermons).